MAHARAN...
Sovereign, Soldier, Scholar

MAHARANA KUMBHA
Sovereign, Soldier, Scholar

Har Bilas Sarda

Rupa & Co

Published 2003 by
Rupa & Co
7/16, Ansari Road, Daryaganj,
New Delhi 110 002

Sales Centres:

Allahabad Bangalore Chandigarh Chennai
Dehradun Hyderabad Jaipur Kathmandu
Kolkata Ludhiana Mumbai Pune

All rights reserved.
No part of this publication may be reproduced, stored in a retrieval system, or transmitted, in any form or by any means, electronic, mechanical, photocopying, recording or otherwise, without the prior permission of the publishers.

Typeset Copyright © Rupa & Co., 2003

Typeset in 11/14 Classical Garamond by
Nikita Overseas Pvt Ltd,
1410 Chiranjiv Tower,
43 Nehru Place
New Delhi 110 019

Printed in India by
Gopsons Papers Ltd.
A-14 Sector 60
Noida 201 301

TO
HINDUPATI. ARYAKHAND BHASHKARA,

Sriman Mukatmani, Medpateshwara,

CHHATRAPATI, RAJ RAJESHWARA,

His Highness Maharaja Dhiraj Maharana Sahib Shri

SIR BHOPAL SINGHJI BAHADUR, C.C.S.I.,
OF
UDAIPUR

This short account of the life and achievements of one of the greatest and most illustrious of his great ancestors,

THE EVER VICTORIOUS MAHARANA KUMBHA,
IS BY KIND PERMISSION,
DEDICATED.

Contents

The Guhilot Family of Mewar	1
Rana Khshetra Singh and Lakhsh Singh	4
Maharana Mokal	18
Kumbha Ascends the Throne	27
Rise and Fall of the Kingdoms of Gujarat and Malwa	32
Maharana's Conquest of Malwa and Capture of Sultan Mahmud Khilji	37
Assassination of Rao Rān Mal and Maharana's Occupation of Marwar	44
Rao Jodhā Recovers Marwar	53
Conquest of Abu and Haravati	59
Wars with the Sultans of Malwa and Gujarat	65
Death of Maharana Kumbha	81
Kumbha's Achievements	85
Kumbha's Monuments	91
Kumbha as a Scholar	121

Inscriptions and Coins	126
Kumbha as a Sovereign	140
Appendix	151
Bibliography	173

Foreword

The first edition of this book was published in A.D. 1917. The present work is practically a new book: many new chapters have been added, and old chapters have been re-written and enlarged.

The accounts of the life and times of Maharana Kumbhakaran of Mewar and his immediate predecessors given in this book, are based principally on old inscriptions and contemporary records.

The more important of the inscriptions of Maharana Kumbha's time are described in Chapter XV; but for facility of reference, I have given in the Appendix (pp. 205–224) the full text of the Rānpur *Chaumukha* Temple Inscription, and all portions of (a) the Kumbhalgarh, (b) the Chitorgarh *Kirtisthambha*, (c) the Shringirishi, (d) the Eklingji Temple and (e) the Samiddeshwar Temple Inscriptions, and (f) the *Eklinga Mahatmya*, to which references have been made in the various chapters of the book. Many of these are being published for the first time.

In writing this book, I have left untapped no source of information available at the present time. I have examined, in the light of inscriptions, coins and contemporary records, the accounts given in the Persian and Hindi histories of the events that occurred during the period with which the book deals. The following pages give an accurate account of the life of Maharana Kumbha as disclosed by these sources of information.

Colonel James Tod's monumental work, *The Annals and Antiquities of Rajasthan,* published in A.D. 1829–32, was written at a time when the history of Rajputana was practically a sealed book to the public. A century has since passed, yet such are the intrinsic merits of 'that wonderful work,' that it still remains the chief source in the English language, to which a student of Rajput history has to turn for enlightenment and knowledge. It is a book which should be read by everyone who belongs to Rajputana or who has Rajput blood in his veins. It should be taught to the students of the Mayo College, Ajmer, and in schools in the Rajput States. Copies of it should be freely given as prize books.

Rajputana has produced several remarkable men, who, by their character and achievements, have made the name *Rajput*, a synonym of chivalry and heroism, and the history of this province is the brightest page in the history of Mediæval India. Their heroic lives and chivalrous deeds are a source of perennial inspiration and interest to Indians.

My sincere obligations are due to Mahamahopadhyaya Pandit Gauri Shankar Ojha, whose unique knowledge of Indian History and vast collection of epigraphic finds have always been available to me. I have received most valuable assistance from him in preparing the Appendix.

The illustration of Maharana Kumbha which appears as Frontispiece to this book is from a photographic copy of an old portrait taken away from Mewar and deposited in the British Museum, London.

Ajmer,   **HAR BILAS SARDA**
1 October 1932

One

The Guhilot Family of Mewar

Maharana Kumbhakaran or Kumbha, as he is popularly called, was one of the greatest of the sovereigns who had ruled in Rajputana. The *Surya Vamsha* is the most famous of the ruling families of India, and the most celebrated of its many branches is the Guhilot family, which has ruled Mewar without a break for nearly fourteen centuries. It has produced some of the greatest and most powerful kings that have made the name of Rajputana resplendent in the annals of India.

Inspired by the highest patriotism, ever upholding *Dharma* though surrounded by powerful foes and faced with almost insuperable difficulties, enduring without flinching untold suffering, and overcoming all by a self-sacrifice and heroism which have wrung the highest praise from their bitterest foes, they have made the pages of history a continuous record of high inspiration and noble purpose. Their immortal deeds, their chivalrous character, their high

2 MAHARANA KUMBHA

ideals, their elevated and noble patriotism have placed them at the head of the Hindu nation and earned for them the title of *Hindua Suraj*, 'the Sun of the Hindus.'

"It has rarely occurred in any country," says Col. Tod, "to have possessed successively so many energetic princes as ruled Mewar through several centuries."[1] Jaitra Singh, Hammir, Kumbhá, Sángá, Pratáp, Ráj Singh are names that will shine bright throughout the ages, and will be revered so long as chivalry is not despised, patriotism not discarded, and valour not condemned.

Maharana Kumbha ascended the throne of Mewar[2] in A.D. 1433 in the renowned fortress of Chitor, and ruled till A.D. 1468, a period of nearly 35 years, which is one of the most prosperous and important in the history of Mewar. His character and achievements are thus summed up in a sentence by Colonel Tod. He says: "All that was wanting to augment her (Mewar's) resources against the storms which were collecting on the brows of Caucasus and the shores of Oxus, and were destined to burst on the head of his grandson, Sángá, was effected by Kumbha, who with Hammir's energy, Lakha's taste for arts, and a genius comprehensive as either and more

---

1. Tod's *Annals and Antiquities of Rajasthan*, Vol. I, p. 287.
2. Colonel Tod, in his *Annals and Antiquities of Rajasthan*, Vol. I, p. 286, gives S. 1475 (A.D. 1419) as the year of Kumbha's accession to the throne. This is incorrect. The Chitor Samiddheshwar Temple Inscription of Magh Sud 3rd, S. 1485 (A.D. 1429) says that Maharana Mokal renovated that temple in A.D. 1429. See Infra p. 13. Barva Devidan's *bahi* gives A.D. 1433 as the year of Kumbha's accession to the throne.

fortunate, succeeded in all his undertakings, and once more raised the crimson banner of Mewar upon the banks of the Caggar, the scene of Samarsi's defeat."[3]

Kumbhá was the eldest son of Ráná Mokal by his Parmár Queen, Sobhágya Devi,[4] daughter of Rájá son of Jaitmál Sánkhla,[5] and thus united in himself the fine qualities of these two of the royal races of India, the culture of the one and the chivalry of the other.

---

3. Tod's *Annals and Antiquities of Rajasthan*, Vol. I, p. 287.
4. Chitorgarh *Kirtisthambha Inscription*, verse 179. Also Kumbhalgarh Inscription of Kumbha. As a girl she was called Maya Kanwar.
5. *See* Kaviraj Bankey Das' Historical Miscellany: No. 450 and 1340. He was ruler of Rūnkot in Marwar.

Two

Rana Khshetra Singh and Lakhsh Singh

Maharana Kumbhá's great-grandfather Rana Khshetra Singh, who ruled Mewar from A.D. 1364 to 1382, was the eldest son and successor of the celebrated Ráná Hammir. Hammir died in A.D. 1364 leaving 4 sons,[1] Khshetra Singh, Luna, Khangār and Aerisal. Khshetra Singh popularly called Kheta,[2] during his 18 years of reign was constantly engaged in warfare. He greatly enlarged the kingdom of Mewar. He captured Ajmer, Jahāzpur, Mandsaur, and annexed *Chhappan*[3] to Mewar. He conquered Hārāvati, the territory

---

1. Mehta Nainsi's *Khyat*.
2. Khshetra Singh was popularly called Khetā, as his son Lakhsh Singh was called Lākha. Maharana Kumbhakaran was popularly called Kumbha and Rana Jaitra Singh was called Jaitā.
3. Tod's *Rajasthan*, Vol. I, p. 42. The southern portion of Mewar is called Chhappan. It formerly belonged to Rathods.

of the Hāras, the principal branch of the Chauhān Rajputs, and took possession of their important fortress Māndalgarh.

The Khumbhalgarh Inscription of A.D. 1460, verse 198, and the *Eklingji*[4] Temple Inscription of A.D. 1488, sl. 131, both say that Khshetra Singh invaded the land of the Hāras, broke and reduced to submission the fortress of Mandalgarh, which according to the *Shringirishi* Inscription of A.D. 1428, even Allauddin Khilji was unable to touch.

Khshetra Singh attacked and defeated the Sultans of Malwa and Gujarat. He defeated Dilawar Khan Ghori, the first Sultan of Malwa in a battle fought as *Bakrole*[5] and destroyed his army. Amin Shah[6] was the original name of Sultan Dilawar Khan Ghori of Malwa, *vide* Rizaqulla Mushtaqi's *Wakiat Mushtaqi*[7] and *Roger's Tuzaki Jahangiri*[8] Dilawar Khan's son's name before he succeeded his father as Sultan of Malwa under the title of Hoshang, was Alpkhan.

The Kumbhalgarh Inscription of A.D. 1460, verse 200, says that the "Mussalman king of Malwa received such a chastisement from Rana Khshetra Singh that he constantly

---

4. Bhavanagar Inscriptions, p. 119.
5. Bakrole was given by Rana Ari Singh as Jagir to Dhiraj Singh, who named the place Hammirgarh, after Rana Ari Singh's successor, Hammir Singh.
6. Some historians have been misled by Amin Shah having become Humayun Shah in some manuscripts. This explains Colonel Tod's statement that the Maharana defeated Emperor Humayun at Bakrole.
7. Elliot's *History of India*, Vol., IV, p. 552.
8. Vol. I, p. 407.

sees him in his dreams." "The Rana captured Amin Shah as a serpent captures a toad," v. 202. The Eklingji Temple Inscription,[9] v. 119, of A.D. 1488, says: "He who burnt down the poison of the pride of the great serpent Amin Shah, was the great Rana Khshetra Singh of Chitor."

The Shringirishi Inscription of A.D. 1428 (unpublished) verse 6, says that Khshetra Singh "by the strength of his sword defeated Amin Shah[10] and killed all the Muslims (of his army) and captured his treasure and countless horses and brought them to Chitor." The *Eklinga Mahatmya*, Sloka 156, and Kumbhá's *Kirtisthambha* Inscription of A.D. 1460 also mention this fact.

The Chitor *Kiritisthambha* Inscription, verse 23, of A.D. 1460, says that Khshetra Singh conquered Idar and imprisoned its valorous ruler Raja Rān Mal, who had completely defeated Zafar Khan, the first independent Sultan of *Gujarat*.[11] The Kumbhalgarh Inscription, verse 196, says "Raja Rān Mal had broken the power of Zafar Khan, who had imprisoned many Rajas. That Rān Mal (Raja of Idar) who had made large numbers of Muslim women widows, had to remain without a bed in Khshetra Singh's prison, when a hundred Rajas were imprisoned."

---

9. Bhavanagar Inscription, p. 119.
10. A couplet in a popular *Rupak* says:—
    एतलो कटक अमीशाह को, खेतल भंजे खड्गबल।
    अइवेग वलन्तो दीठ में, रहस तरोवर एक तल ॥
    — Nainsi's *Khyat*, p. 22.
11. Lane Poole's *Muhammadan Dynasties of India*, p. 312.

The Eklingji Temple Inscription, v. 119, of A.D. 1485, says that the Maharana took away the State treasure of Idar and placed Rān Mal's son on the throne of that kingdom.

The Kumbhalgarh Inscription, v. 119, says that Khshetra Singh conquered Toda, defeating its ruler *Satal*.[12]

Rana Khshetra Singh died in A.D. 1382, leaving 7 sons, of whom the eldest Lakhsh Singh succeeded him. Only one inscription of the time of Khshetra Singh has so far come to light. It is engraved on the door of the *Seetla Mata* temple in Gogandā and is dated the Asoj Vad 13, V. S. 1423 (A.D. 1366).

RANA LAKHSH SINGH

Lakhsh Singh or Lakha,[13] as he was popularly called, was one of the most successful of the Maharanas of Mewar, and reigned from A.D. 1382 to 1397. In his father Rana Khshetra Singh's time, while he was heir apparent to the throne, Lakhā led an expedition against the fortress of Joga[14] and conquered it.

He extended his dominions by the subjugation of Merwārā. He destroyed the chief strong-hold of the Mérs, Beratgarh, on the ruins of which he founded Badnor.[15] The Kumbhalgarh Inscription of S. 1460, V. 212, and the

---

12. For an account of Todā, see Archaeological Survey Report for 1872–73, Vol. VI, p. 124.
13. Also called Lākhan.
14. Eklingji Temple Inscription, V. 35, published in Bhavanagar Inscriptions, p. 119.
15. Tod's Rajasthan, Vol. 1, p. 274.

Chitorgarh Tower of Victory Inscription, verse 36, mention this conquest. It was during his reign that the tin and silver mines of Jawār in the hilly district of Mewar were discovered. With the revenues thus augmented, he rebuilt the palaces and temples which had been destroyed by Sultan Allauddin Khilji of Delhi. He excavated many reservoirs and lakes, raised immense ramparts to dam their waters and constructed a number of forts.[16]

Tradition has it that during Rana Lakha's reign, a rich *Banjara* constructed the famous Picholā lake, on the bank of which the city of Udaipur was built later. This beautiful lake containing the celebrated island palaces of Jagmandir and Jagniwas, is 2½ miles long by 1½ miles wide. It was in one of the Jagmandir palaces that Shahjahan, then Prince Khurram, was given shelter by Maharana Karan Singh when the former rebelled against his father Emperor Jahāngir in A.D. 1622. The Maharana built a domed building for the prince, the interior being decorated with mosaics in onyx cornelian jaspers and agates while a chapel was built nearby to a Muslim saint to keep the Prince in the odour of sanctity. Maybe that Shah Jahan here got the idea of marble mosaics for the famous *Taj Bibi ka Roza* or Taj Mahal that he built at Agra.

Inscriptions of the time of Maharana Lakha show that Ghanérao, Nānā and Kot Solankian had become incorporated with Mewar. The inscription dated V.S. 1468 (A.D. 1411) engraved on the magnificent steel *trisula* in the Achaleshwar

---

16. *Vir Vinod*, Vol. 1, p. 308.

temple at Abu, says that the *trisula* had been manufactured in Ghanérao in Maharana Lakha's time. Another inscription of V.S. 1475 (A.D. 1419) found in Kot Solankian says that the Jain temple in the Asalpur fort was renovated in Maharana Lākhā's time, *Vide* Muni Jin Vijai's *Prāchin Lekh Sangrah*, Part II, p. 221, Inscription no. 370. These two inscriptions show that the rich province of Godwar had passed into the Maharana's possession either in Lakha's time or before it.

Rana Lakha conquered the Sankhlā Rajputs of Shekhāwāti (Nagarchal[17] territory), and like his father, defeated the royal army of the Sultan of Delhi at Badnor, and the Sultan of Gujarat at Mandalgarh.[18] He liberated *Tristhali*[19] (Benares, Allahabad and Gaya) from the Mussalmans and the hill fort of Vardhan[20] from the Meds (Mérs). Col. Tod says: "He carried the war to Gaya, and in driving the barbarian from this sacred place, lost his life."[21]

---

17. *Vir Vinod*, p. 306. Also Tod's *Rajasthan*, Vol. 1, p. 274.
18. Ferishta (Vol. IV, p. 6) says that Sultan Muzaffar Shah of Gujarat invaded Mandalgarh in A.D. 1396, but returned without conquering it, as he was given gold and jewels. The Mussalman historians generally describe defeats of Mussalman kings by saying that the Sultan returned owing to the rainy season having set in, or, because he was given gold and jewels. Gujarat histories make no mention of this expedition against Mandalgarh. *The Mirati Sikandari* mentions Mandu by mistake for Mandalgarh—Bayley's Gujarat, p. 77.
19. Maharana Kumbha's Kumbhalgarh Inscription, V. 207 (Also Chitorgarh *Kirtisthambha* Inscription, V. 3).
20. *Ibid*, V. 36.
21. *Annals and Antiquities of Rajasthan*, Vol. 1, p. 275.

10 MAHARANA KUMBHA

It was about this time, the close of the fourteenth century, A.D., that the Rathods, who under their leader Sihaji, had come in the thirteenth century A.D., from the United Provinces, and settled in Pali (Marwar), began to take root in the congenial soil of this hospitable region, and throw out ramifications all round. One branch had settled in Mālāni, where the famous warrior, Mallinath ruled. Mallinath had attained the position of a *Siddha*, *i.e.* one who by his religious pieties and practices had become perfect. Mallinath's son Jugmal was also a hero[22] and his romantic career is remembered to this day by the deeds of chivalry he performed, and which are sung throughout Rajputana.

Sihaji who died[23] on *Kartik Vad* 12, S. 1330 (A.D. 1273) was the son of Setkumar Rathod and was succeeded by his son Asthān, who was succeeded by Duhad, then Raipal, then

---

22. Gindoli, the daugther of the ruler of Gujarat having heard of the heroic deeds of Jugmal fell in love with him, and Jugmal coming to know of it, brought away the girl, and refused to restore her.

    गोदोली बांधी गलै, जका न दे जगमाल

    The ruler of Gujarat invaded Jugmal's territory but was defeated and had to return discomfited. The popular couplet:—

    बीबी पूछे खान ने, जग केता जगमाल

    "The Begam asks the Khan 'how many Jugmals are there in the world" (meaning that apparently the world is full of them) shows the brave deeds of the Rajputs in the war. This war is laid to have continued for six months. A song commemorating the love of Jugmal and Gindoli, Jugmal's refusal to give up Gindoli, and his valorous deeds in the war are sung in Rajputana, particularly accompanied by the *Ghumar* dance.

23. His *Samadha* (mausoleum) was built by his widow Solankini Parvati, *vide Indian Antiquary*, Vol. 40, p. 301.

Kampal, after whom came Jalansi, then Chhada and then Tida, followed by Sulkha and Viram. Viram was killed by the Joiya Rajputs, and his son Chondā becoming homeless, passed his childhood in the service of a Brahmin, looking after his cows. In early youth, however, he gathered a following and defeated the Joiyas, recovered his patrimony and eventually won distinction as the first Rathod King of Marwar, with Mandor as his Capital.

Marwar had, for centuries, been ruled by Pratihar Rajputs. In the 14th century A.D., their power had greatly declined owing to the constant inroads of the Mussalman governors of Nagor in the north-east, and the Chauhans of Jalor in the south-west. As the Pratihar Chief, Inda Raidhawal was unequal to the burdens of the sovereignty of Marwar during these troublous time, he gave his daughter in marriage to Chondā, as he and his supporters thought that the enterprising Chondā would be able to save the country from falling into the hands of the Mussalmans of Nagor. With the princess was given the kingdom of Mandor in dowry, and it was stipulated that Chondā would keep the Pratihar nobles in possession of their several estates. A couplet referring to this event, says:—

इंदां रो उपकार कमधज मत भूलै कदै।
चुँडो चँवरी चाड दियो मंडावर डायजे ॥

"Rathods, never forget the great
benefit, Indas[24] hve conferred.
Chondā was married: Mandor was
given in dowry (to him)."

---

24. Indas are a branch of Pratihar Rajputs.

Chintamani V. Vaidya in his *History of Mediæval Hindu India*, says: "The Rathods first took shelter under the Pratihars of Mandor whom they subsequently treacherously supplanted."[25] This sentence contains two allegations: (1) that the Rathods took shelter under the Pratihars of Mandor and (2) that the Rathods subsequently treacherously supplanted them in the land. He has, however, nowhere quoted any authority or given any reasons whatever to support these allegations, which are absolutely unfounded. The learned author thus describes[26] the advent of the Rathods in Rajputana:— "In fact, throughout Indian history, Rajputana appears to have afforded a sheltering ground to the Indo-Aryans, whenever they were thrust out of their richer lands, blessed with plentiful water, by barbarian hordes like the Sakas, the Kushans, the Huns and lastly the Muhammadan Turks and Afghans. The last of the Rajput families which thus took shelter in the sands of Rajasthan, we know from authentic history, were the Rathods of Kanauj, who after the defeat and death of Jayachand came from the Gangetic valley to the sands of Marwar."

Though the word shelter is used here, yet it has no connection with the Pratihars of Mandor. Vaidya simply says that the Rathods took shelter in Rajputana from the inroads and invasions of the Turks and the Afghans, by emigrating from Kanauj to Marwar. He nowhere says that the Pratihars of Mandor actually gave or promised to give the immigrant

---

25. Vol. II, p. 99.
26. Vol. II, p. 68.

RANA KHSHETRA SINGH AND LAKHSH SINGH

Rathods any protection or help. As a matter of fact historical records show that during a pilgrimage of Sihaji to Pushkar, the inhabitants of Bhinmal and Pali asked Sihaji to settle in Pali and protect them from the Muslim raids from Sindh and Nagor. Later, he describes the rise and fall of the Pratihars of Kanauj including the branch at Mandor, but does not say when and in what way the Rathods treacherously supplanted the Pratihars. No responsible historian has ever asserted that the Rathods under Chondā or someone else wrested Mandor from the Pratihars by treachery. The fact is that the Pratihars of Mandor had become very weak by constant warfare, defending themselves against the Mussalmans of Nagor on one side and the Chauhans of Jalor on the other; and when they found that they could no longer stand these inroads, they allied themselves to the rising Rathod Power led by the enterprising Chondā and very wisely handed over the defence of their land to their relations, the Rathods.

There was no question of treachery or unfair dealing of any kind. On the contrary, if the Pratihars had not entrusted the protection of Mandor to Rathod Chondā, the probabilities are that Mandor would have fallen into the hands of the Muslim rulers of Nagor.

Not only did Chondā consolidate his kingdom, keeping off the Muslims of Nagor, but succeeded eventually in subjugating them and taking possession of their capital Nagor.

Rao Chondā had 14 sons, the eldest being Rān Mal. Chondā, however, was very fond of his Mohil Queen, and wishing to give the kingdom to her son Kānha, made his wish known to Rān Mal. Rān Mal, to respect his father's wishes, left Mandor[27] with 500 horsemen and went to Chitor, where

14 MAHARANA KUMBHA

Maharana Lakha bestowed a jagir of 40 villages on him. Rao Chondā died in A.D. 1410, and Kānha succeeded him at Mandor.

Many years before his death, while Maharana Lakha was still adorning the throne of Mewar and embelishing the country, an incident occurred, which, while it illustrates the thoughtless character of the Rajput, gave rise to an event which compromised the right of primogeniture to the throne of Mewar, and in the words of Colonel Tod, "proved more disastrous in its consequences than the arms of either Mughals or Mahrattas."

Lakha was advanced in years, and his sons established in suitable domains, when the coconut came from the Rao of Mandawar (Mandor) to affiance his daughter Hansbai, Rān Mal's sister, to the heir of Mewar. "When the embassy was announced, Rān Mal was present in the Durbar; but Chonda, the heir of Mewar, was absent, and the old chief was seated in his chair of state surrounded by his court. The messenger of hymen was courteously received by Lakha, who observed that Chondā would soon return and take the gage; "for," added he, drawing his fingers over his moustachios, "I do not suppose, you send such playthings to an old grey-beard like me." This little sally was applauded and repeated. Chondā offended at delicacy being sacrificed to wit, declined to accept the symbol, which his father had even in jest supposed might

---

27. Mehta Nainsi (*Khyat*, p. 23, Benares edition) says that Rao Chondā at the request of his Mohil queen ordered Rān Mal to go into exile and that several brave Rajputs espoused his cause and went away with him to Chitor.

be intended for himself."[28] Thinking that his father still had a secret longing for married life, Chondā made up his mind that Lakha should himself accept the symbol. He asked Rān Mal, who happened to be at Chitor at the time, to invite him to a feast, and there he insisted on Rān Mal agreeing to give his sister to the Maharana before joining his festive board. Rān Mal would not agree to this and the night neared the morn with the festive board still deserted.

Not knowing how else to get out of the difficulty, Rān Mal hit on a proposal which he thought would turn the tables on Chonda. He suggested through *Charan* Chandan Khadiya that Chonda should renounce his right to the throne of Chitor in favour of an issue of the Rana by Rān Mal's sister. The magnanimous Chonda whose sole desire was to gratify the supposed wish of his father, unhesitatingly agreed to this. The marriage was celebrated and Mokal was the issue of this union.

When Mokal was still a minor, "Lakha resolved to signalise his finale by a raid against the enemies of his faith and to expel the barbarian from the holy land of Gaya. When war was made against their religion by the Tatar proselytes of Islam, the Sutlaj and the Caggar were as the banks of the Jordan—Gaya, their Jerusalem, their holy land; and if the destiny filled his cup, the Hindu chieftain was secure of his beatitude (Moksha) and borne from the scene of probation in celestial cars by the Apsaras, was introduced at once into the realm of the Sun. Ere, however, the Rana of Chitor

---

28. Mehta Nainsi gives a slightly different account of this incident; *see* his *Khyat*, p. 23.

journeyed to this bourne, he was desirous of leaving his throne unexposed to civil strife. The subject of succession had never been renewed, but discussing with Chonda his war-like pilgrimage to Gaya, from which he might not return, he sounded him by asking what estates should be settled on Mokal. The 'Throne of Chitor' was the honest reply; and to set suspicions at rest, he desired that the ceremony of installation should be performed previous to Lakha's departure Chonda was the first to pay homage and swear obedience and fidelity to his future sovereign.[29]

Lakha had the Holy-land freed[30] from the yoke of the Afghan but lost his life in the enterprise. When news of this event reached Chitor, Mohal's mother prepared to become *Sati*. Chonda appeared and dissuaded her from her resolution saying that Mokal was a child, and she, the Queenmother, must watch over the welfare of the Rana. The Queen had not expected this steadfast fidelity from Chonda. She praised his unexampled conduct and declared that he (Chonda) should ever have the first place in the Council, and no grant by the Rana should take effect till it was confirmed by him. This is still maintained, and in all grants the lance of the Salumbra still precedes the monogram of the Rana."[31]

---

29. Tod's *Rajasthan*, Vol. I, p. 277.
30. The *Kirtisthambha Inscription*, Vol. 31 simply says that the Maharana liberated Gaya from Muslim tax.
31. In old days all *grants* were written in Sanskrit and signed by the King. But Maharana Kumbha discontinued signing grants. Henceforth, instead of the signature, only the word सही confirmed began to be written by the Maharana.

This assignment of the first place in the council and a recognition of the premier position amongst the vassalage of Mewar, became the cause of its ruin, when, in the 18th century, the decendants of Chonda strenuously worked to maintain the position thus assigned to Chonda, but forgot the self-sacrifice of that great man, and proved incapable of following in the footsteps of the illustrious founder of their family, when their country had need of those qualities of head and heart, which are so gloriously illustrated in the life of Chonda.

Rana Lakhsh Singh died some time between A.D. 1419 and A.D. 1421. A stone inscription[32] found in Kot Solankian in the Godwar district of Marwar says that the Paraswanath temple in the Asalpur fort was renovated on Monday the *Asar Sud* 3rd, S. 1475 (A.D. 1419) during the victorious reign of Rana Laksh Singh. The earliest inscription of the time of his son and successor Mokal, is dated the *Pos Sud* 6, S. 1478 (A.D. 1421). This shows that Rana Lakhsh Singh died sometime after the year A.D. 1419 and before A.D. 1421, in which year Mokal the youngest of Lakha's sons,[33] was reigning in Mewar.

---

32. Muni Jinvijaya's *Prachin Jain Lekh Sangrah*, part II, p. 221, inscription No. 370. The Asar, S. 1475, of the Mewar State Sambat corresponds with the *Chaitra*, S. 1476 of the ordinary Vikrama era.
33. Maharana Lakhsh Singh had nine sons, Chonda, Raghavadeva, Ajja, Uda, Dula, Gajsingh, Dungersingh, Manda and Mokal, Nainsi's *Khyat*, p. 25, omits Ajja.

Three

Maharana Mokal

As Mokal, when he ascended the throne, was very young, Chonda was at the head of affairs in Mewar. His high character, love of justice, and utter unselfishness made the administration most efficient and won the admiration and love of the people. The Queenmother of Chitor, Hansbai, was young and inexperienced, and interested parties began to poison her ears. The intrigue developed, and Hansbai became apprehensive because of the predominant influence of Chonda. At last, one day she sent for Chonda and said that either he should leave Mewar, or some place be fixed where she would retire with her minor son Mokal. The chivalrous Chonda, who had willingly renounced the throne of Chitor in favour of Mokal, determined to leave Mewar and told her that he was leaving Chitor immediately and asked her to look after Mewar carefully. Apprehensive of the designs of the unscrupulous people round the Queenmother, Chonda asked his younger brother Rāghavadeva to watch over the young Maharana, and himself went away with his brother Ajja and others to Māndu, where the Sultan received him with open arms and granted him the district of Hallar as jagir.[1]

After Chonda's departure, Rān Mal, the brother of Hansbai, became her chief adviser and the Rathods were given high offices and jagirs in Mewar. But events occurred in Mandor which sent Ran Mal back to Marwar.

On the death of Rao Chonda of Mandor in A.D. 1410, his son Kānha had succeeded him, the eldest son Rān Mal having renounced his claim to the throne in favour of Kānha in deference to his father's wishes.

Kānha after ruling Marwar for some years died without leaving a son. Kānha's eldest brother Rān Mal was in Chitor and Satta and Randhir, his other two elder brothers were in Mandor. Randhir, the youngest of the three brothers, asked Satta what would be given to Randhir if the latter put Satta on the throne instead of Rān Mal, the eldest of them all. Satta promised to give half the territory to Randhir. Randhir placed Satta on the throne himself getting half the estate. But he had not counted with Narbad, the war-like son of Satta, who did not like that half the income of Marwar should go to Randhir. Narbad determined to get rid of Randhir. Randhir's son Napa soon died of poison, and one Dayal having apprised Randhir of his impending doom, Randhir repaired to Chitor and instigated Rān Mal to claim his patrimony.[2] Both Satta and

---

1. Tod's *Rajasthan*, Vol. I, p. 278.
2. See *Vir Vinod*, p. 312.

Rān Mal were maternal uncles of the Maharana Mokal, but as Rān Mal was the rightful successor of Kānha, the Maharana expoused his cause and furnished him with a large army, with which he invaded Mandor, defeated Satta and recovered his rightful inheritance. The Maharana called Satta and Narbad to Chitor and bestowed a jagir of a lakh of rupees with the town of Kāyalānā on Narbad and enrolled him among his vassals. Rān Mal thus began to reign in Mandor.[3]

Mokal's short reign of about 13 years—he came to the throne about the year A.D. 1420 and was assassinated in A.D. 1433—was full of great events. He maintained the traditions of the House by inflicting a defeat on Muhammad Tughlaq, the King of Delhi, in the field of Raipur. Maharana Mokal "overran Sapādalaksha (Ajmer) territory and took Sāmbhar from the Sultan of Delhi." The *Kumbhalgarh Inscription* of the time of Maharana Kumbha, dated Monday the 3rd of November, A.D. 1460, says that "the ruler of Jalor (Jabalipur) trembled before him, and the King of Delhi became anxious about his territory."

A principality subordinate to Gujarat had been established at Nagor about A.D. 1404 by Shams Khan, who was succeeded by his son Firoz Khan. The Samiddheshwar Mahadeva Temple Inscription of *Magh Sud* 3rd, S. 1485 (A.D. 1429) says that "Maharana Mokal invaded Nagor and defeated Sultan Firoz Khan. Firoz Khan's two sons, Modood and Masti and

---

3. Mehta Nainsi in his *Khyat* (p. 25) says that after recovering Mandor with the help of Maharana Mokal's army, Rān Mal gave Mandor to his eldest son Jodhá and himself took up residence at Nagor.

his numerous elephants were killed in the battle."[4] The Khan of Nagor accepted Maharana Mokal's suzereinty, and in acknowledgment of its used to send all colts born in Nagor to the Maharana's stables at Chitor.[5] The *Shringirishi Inscription* of A.D. 1428 (V.S. 1485) says that Padshah Ahmad (of Gujarat) was defeated by Mokal and had to flee for his life, leaving his treasure behind. Also, *Kumbhalgarh Inscription* of A.D. 1460 says that both Firoz and Muhammad (Ahmad) were defeated and had to flee for their lives. The *Eklingji Temple Inscription*,[6] V. 44, of A.D. 1488, of the time of Maharana Raimal says that Maharana Mokal obtained a victory at Jahazpur over Firoz Khan.

Mokal re-built the great temple of Samiddeshwar Mahadeva[7] near the 'Tower of Victory' at Chitor and made a grant of Dhanpur for its upkeep; and gave the villages of Bándanwara (now in the Ajmer District) and Ramgaon (2 miles from *Eklingji*) for the upkeep of the *Eklingji* temple. He constructed a beautiful tank at *Pāpamochana Tirtha*.[8] He also built the Dwarkanath temple at Chitor with the tank attached to it.

---

4. Mehta Nainsi's *Khyat*, p. 26, foot-note.
5. Kaviraj Bankey Das' *Miscellany of Historical Records:* Record No. 943.
6. Bhavanagar Inscriptions, p. 120.
7. This temple was originally built by Raja Bhoja, the famous Paramra King of Dhar, and was called Tribhuvan Narain Temple after Bhoja's surname, Tribhuvan Narain.
8. He presented a temple of Devi with an image of a lion made of *Sarvadhat* (all the metals) and a temple of Vishnu with a gold image of Garuda. *Vide, Kumbhalgarh Inscription.*

"He overcame the Nishadas (Bhils) and struck terror into the hearts of the Turushkas (Muslims)." An inscription in the temple of Mokalji at Chitor, v. 46, of S. 1485 (A.D. 1428) published in the *Epigraphia Indica*, Vol. II, p. 416, says: "He (Mokal) extirpated the Nishads and conquered the Turushkas (Mussalmans)." He went on pilgrimage to Dwarka and Sankhoddhāra.[9]

Maharana Mokal built the high wall (*Kot*) round the *Eklingji* temple[10] with its three gates. He constructed a tank in memory of his Bagheli queen Gaurambika[11] at *Shringirishi* at Chitor, and the Baghela tank after the name of his brother Bagh Singh,[12] who had died childless. Mokal gave 24 gold and silver *tuladān*, a gold *tuladān* being given in the Varāh Temple at Pushkar.[13] He established a seminary to teach the Vedas[14] to the Brahmins who had taken to agriculture.

In A.D. 1433, the Maharana left Chitor to quell a revolt of the hill tribes in his dominions. While he was encamped at Madaria, a deputation came from the Chief of Gagroon requesting immediate help in fulfilment of a promise given by the Maharana at the marriage of his daughter. Besides seven sons, Mokal had a daughter named Lalbai,[15] who had

---

9. *Raja Prasasti*, Canto IV.
10. *Shringirishi Inscription*, V. 16.
11. *Shringirishi Inscription*, V. 16.
12. *Kumbhalgarh Inscription* of A.D. 1460. Also *Raja Prasanti*, Canto IV.
13. *Kumbhalgarh Inscription* of A.D. 1460.
14. Kumbhalgarh Inscription of A.D. 1460.
15. Kaviraj Bankeydas in his *Miscellany* gives her name as *Pushpawati*.

MAHARANA MOKAL

been married to Achal Singh, the Kheechi Chief of Gagroon. Achal Singh had at the *Hathleva* demanded and received from the Maharana the pledge of succour on invasion of his territory. As Sultan Hoshang of Malwa, attacked Gagroon, Achal Singh sent his son Dhiraj Singh to the Maharana demanding fulfilment of his pledge. As the Maharana was preparing to go towards Gagroon, news arrived that Sultan Ahmad Shah of Gujarat had passed through Dungerpur and had begun to demolish temples in Jheelwara in Mewar. Mokal started to drive the Sultan out of Mewar. The *Vir Vinod* says that in A.D. 1432, Ahmad Shah, the King of Gujarat started with a large army on a conquering expedition, and passing through Jheelwara (part of Mewar) began to plunder the country and break temples, and that the Maharana hearing of this, started at once to attack Ahmad Shah. He was, however, prevented from going to Gagroon or driving out the Sultan by an incident which cost the Maharama his life, and which throws a lurid light on the character of the Rajputs.

In the army of the Maharana there were two natural sons of Rana Khshetra Singh by a handsome girl named Karmān, daughter of Mednimal carpenter—a class well-known for the physical beauty of their women. They were named Chacha and Maira, and had risen to be captains in the army of Maharana Mokal. Some of the chiefs of Mewar, jealous of their rise, wished to humiliate them and had recourse to a trick which resulted in the assassination of the Maharana.

One day, while the Maharana was encamped at Madaria and was seated in a grove with his chiefs around him, he enquired the name of a particular tree. Hārā Māldeva, feigning ignorance wispered to him to ask either of the brothers. Not perceiving the insinuation involved in the question, Mokal turned to the brothers and artlessly asked "Kakaji (uncle) what tree is this?" The question reminded them of their mother's origin and was taken to be an insult.

They conspired to murder the Maharana, and won over Mahipal Panwar popularly called Mahpa and some other minor chiefs to their cause. They, however, failed to gain over Malesi *Dodiya*,[16] brother of Shalji. News of the conspiracy reached Rān Mal and he warned the Maharana that an attempt on his life was imminent. Sanwaldas, the Raja of Idar, who had come with his army to aid the Maharana in his attack on the King of Gujarat came to know of the plot owing to his intimacy with Chacha and warned Mokal, but Mokal only laughed at the idea just as he had taken no heed of Rān Mal's warning.

An occasion soon presented itself to the traitors for carrying into execution their nefarious design. One night while the Maharana was encamped at Bāgor, the two traitors, collecting a small force, surprised the Maharana in his tents. The Maharana's attendants prepared to defend him. Nine men stood by the Maharana, five by his Queen Hadiji and five by Malesi Dodiya, the gatekeeper of the palace. The Maharana, Rani Hadiji and Malesi defended themselves bravely but were killed, not however, till they had slain 19 of the conspirators and wounded Chacha and Mahpa. Seventy of the Maharana's men, including Sanwaldas, were slain. The Maharana's eldest son Kumbha escaped with difficulty. Going

---

16. Dodiya is the head of the guard at the entrance of a palace.

to the house of a Patel who owned two of the fleetest horses in Mewar, he mounted one and killing the other at the suggestion of the Patel to baffle pursuit, escaped and reached Chitor. The traitors, who were looking out for Kumbha, were at the Patel's house soon after his departure, but seeing one steed lying dead and the other gone, they returned to their tents. The traitors thence went to Chitor but finding the gates shut against them,[17] returned to Madaria and proclaimed Chacha as Maharana of Mewar, Mahpa becoming his Diwan. Finding, however, their position untenable, they fled to the hills of *Pai Kotra* with their families and throwing themselves into the strong-hold of Rātākot, fortified it.

Maharana Mokal left seven sons, Kumbhakaran, Khshemakaran, Shiva, Satta, Nathsingh, Viramdeva, and Rajdhar. Kumbhakaran or Kumbha the eldest of the seven sons succeeded Mokal.

Only four stone inscriptions of Maharana Mokal's time have so far come to light. The first is engraved on the lintel of the Jain temple of Śantinatha at Jāwar and is dated the *Pos Sud* 6th, S. 1478 (A.D. 1421). It is published in *Prachin Lekh Sangrah*, Vol. I, p. 35, Inscription No. 118 (Bhavanagar). The second is in a *tibari* (verandah) in the Shringirishi 6 miles to the south-east of the *Eklingji* Temple and is dated the *Sravan Sud* 5th, S. 1485 (A.D. 1428) A portion of it has disappeared. It was composed by Kaviraj Vanikdas Yogeshwar. A summary of it is published in the Rajputana Museum Report for

---

17. The *Vir Vinod* says that the traitors went to Chitor, brought their families and sought shelter in the hills of Pai Kotra.

A.D. 1925. The third inscription which is dated the *Magh Sud* 3rd, S. 1485 (A.D. 1429) exists in the Samiddheshwar temple at Chitor. It was composed by Bhatta Vishnu's son Aiknath, a *dashora* brahmin. It is published in the Bhavanagar Inscriptions, p. 96.

The fourth inscription, which has come to light only in March this year, is engraved on a stone which has recently been removed from the *Hinglu Vāva* (Hinglu stepped well) near the village of Amberi, 6 miles from Udaipur between that place and *Eklingji*. It is dated Thursday the Jeth Sud, 5th, S. 1487,[18] corresponding with 16th May A.D. 1431. It records the construction of the *Vāva* (well) by a Brahmin in Maharana Mokal's reign.

---

18. Indian Ephemeris by L.D.S. Pallai Vol. V. According to current Vikarma era, the year of the inscription must be S. 1487.

Four

Kumbha Ascends the Throne

Maharana Kumbha ascended the throne of Mewar at Chitor in A.D. 1433. His first care was to punish the traitors Chacha and Maira and their fellow-conspirators. This involved military operations and a war with Mandu.

When the news of the tragedy of Mokal's death reached Rao Rān Mal, the brother of Mokal's mother Hans Bai, this valiant Rathod king, remembering the debt of gratitude he owed to Mokal, with whose help he had recovered the throne of Marwar, threw off the turban he was wearing, put on a *phenta* (a piece of cloth generally worn when in mourning) and swore that he would put the turban on his head only when he had avenged Mokal by slaying his murderers. Leaving Mandor he came to Chitor, showed Nazar to the Maharana and with 500 horsemen started in pursuit of the traitors towards the Pái hills. Arriving there, he made several attempts to reach the fortress, but so steep was the hill, and so rugged the path that led up to the fort that Rān Mal failed to achieve his object.

During the reign of Mokal, Rān Mal had, while living at Chitor, killed a Bhil zamindar named Gameti of a village situated at the foot of the Pái hills. The sons of this zamindar with other Bhils, were now actively assisting Chacha and Maira against Rān Mal. Finding that without the assistance of the Bhils he could not reach the fort, Rān Mal went unattended to the house of the Bhil he had murdered. His widow was at home and the sons had gone out. He addressed her as sister, greeted her, and sat down. The Bhil woman said: "Brother, you did us great wrong, but as you have come to our house, we cannot do anything to you now." Hearing the approach of her sons, the Bhil lady asked Rān Mal to go inside the house, and had his horse tethered at the back of it. Her five sons now arrived and sat down to dinner. She asked them what they would do to Rān Mal if he should come to their house. The young men exclaimed, "Do what! We will kill him." The eldest, however, said "Mother, if he comes to our house, we will say nothing to him." The lady praised her son's noble sentiments and called to Rān Mal to come out. Ran Mal came out. The Bhils received him courteously and asked him why he had come there to be killed. He replied: "My dear nephews, I have taken a vow not to eat bread till I have killed Cháchá and Mairá; but with you to assist them, I cannot get at them." The Bhils[1] thus appealed to, promised to abstain from rendering any further assistance to Cháchá and Mairá,

---

1. For an account of the Bhils, see *Gazetteer of Udaipur* p. 227, by Major K.D, Erskine, A.D. 1908.

and to assist Rān Mal in achieving his object. Rān Mal returned to his camp and started next day with 1,140 Guhilots and Rathods to take the fort. On arriving at the foot of the hill, the Bhils advised Rān Mal to wait a few days, as the bypath leading to the fort had been blocked by a lioness who had lately given birth to a cub. Rān Mal said he did not mind that, and went on. Placing his men at suitable points he ascended the hill with 60 men. They commenced the ascent where the parapet was yet low. The path was steep and rugged; and in the darkness of the night each grasped his neighbour's skirt for security. As the party reached a ledge of the rock, the glowing eye-balls of the lioness flashed upon them as she came roaring towards them. Rān Mal ordered his son, Aradakamal, to dispose of the beast. He advanced and buried his poniard in her breast.[2] This omen was superb. They soon reached the summit. Some had ascended the parapet, others were scrambling over when the minstrel slipping, fell, and his drum which was to have accompanied his voice in celebrating the conquest, awoke, by its crash, the daughter of Cháchá. Her father quieted her fears by saying it was the thunder and rain of *bhádon*, and told her to fear God only and go to sleep, for their enemies were safe at Kailwá. At this moment the avengers of Mokal rushed in. Rān Mal hurled his spear at the door, and people at once said it was Rān Mal's. Cháchá and Maira had no time to avoid their

---

2. Another account says that Rān Mal's sword only wounded the lioness, whereupon Chandan Charan, who was with Rān Mal, killed her with a poniard. See foot-note in *Vir Vinod*, p. 318.

fate. Cháchá was cleft in two by Chauhán Sujá,[3] while the Rathod prince laid Mairá at his feet. Rān Mal then went to the quarters occupied by Mahpa Panwár and called him to come out and meet his fate, for he had taken a vow not to attack anyone who was in the company of women. At the very first call, Máhpá, unable to face his foe, put on female garments and thus disguised, left the house unmolested. In answer to the second call, a Dom woman shouted from inside that the Thákur had put on her clothes and left the house and that she was sitting naked inside. On this, Rān Mal returned and joined his companions. Though Chácha and Mairá met the fate they richly deserved, Chácha's son, Ekká, escaped; and he and Máhpá made straight for the Court of Mandu, where they found shelter. Rān Mal took Chácha's daughter to wife, making Chácha's body serve as a *bajot*[4] to sit on at the ceremony.

Chácha and Mairá had captured 500 girls from the villages round about the Pái Hills and kept them in this strong-hold. Rān Mal married these girls there to spears, intending to give them to his Rathod followers. The Maharana's uncle, Raghávadeva, the brother of Chondá, did not like this proposal, and on arriving at Delwara removed the maids to his own camp. This added fuel to the fire of jealousy already existing between Rághavadeva and Rān Mal.

Rao Rān Mal preferring the fertile plateau of Mewar to the arid desert of Marwar took up his residence at Chitor,

---

3. Tod says that Suja was a Chandana Rajput.
4. A round or square wooden seat to squat upon.

and surrounded himself and the Maharana with Rathods, and began to take a prominent part in the administration of Mewar. Rághavadeva, who had been left by his elder brother Chondá, on his departure from Chitor during the reign of the late Maharana Mokal to watch over the safety of the Maharana during his minority, had the same duty to perform now that Maharana Kumbhá, Mokal's son, was young. Rághavadeva did not approve of the proceedings at the Court, which was now dominated by the Rathods, and not willing to do anything which might be unpalatable to the Dowager Maharani, who was Rān Mal's sister, he silently watched the progress of events. But his existence was a menace to the growing influence of the Rathods. It was, therefore, resolved to remove him. One day, he was invited to a Durbar and given a dress of honour. As he was putting it on, his arms became entangled in the sleeves, which had been sewn at the ends, and he was assassinated by two of Rān Mal's men, who stabbed him with their daggers.[5] Rághavadeva had been loved throughout Mewar for his high character, courage, manly beauty and patriotism. This murder roused great indignation against the Rathods, and obtained for the victim divine honours and a place amongst the *Pitridevas* of Mewar.

---

5. *Vir Vinod*, Vol. I, p. 319. Mehta Nainsi's *Khyat* (p. 29) gives a different account.

Five

Rise and Fall of the Kingdoms of Gujarat and Malwa

The invasion of India by Timur, the flight of Muhammad Tughlaq from Delhi, and the conquest and sack of that city by the invader in A.D. 1398, destroyed the power of the Tughlaq Sultans of Delhi. After Timur's departure to Turkistan, Muhammad Tughlaq returned to Delhi, but he had lost all power and prestige, and was a Sultan more in name than in reality. In the opening years of the fifteenth century, Malwa and Gujarat the erstwhile viceroyalties of Delhi threw off their allegiance and declared their independence. Malwa and Gujarat became powerful monarchies, and it was these kingdoms, and the principality of Nagor, then in the heyday of their power and prosperity, that Maharana Kumbhā, about the middle of the fifteenth century, fought and defeated.

GUJARAT

Gujarat had been under the rule of the Baghelá branch of the Chalukya Rajputs till the year A.D. 1297, when Sultan Ala-ud-din Khilji of Delhi sent Ulugh Khan to conquer it. The Chalukyas had succeeded the Cháurá Rajputs, who had founded Anhilwara Pātan, the celebrated Capital of Gujarat. The monarchy of Gujarat reached the height of its magnificence and power under the Solanki monarchs Siddhráj Jaisingh and Kumár Pál (A.D. 1094-1175), when it triumphed over Malwa, conquered Chitor and defeated the Chauhān King Ânnādeva of Ajmer.

Gujarat remained a tributary province of Delhi from A.D. 1297 to the year A.D. 1396, when the Viceroy, Zafar Khan, proclaimed his independence and mounted the throne of Gujarat[1] at Birpur, under the title of Muzaffar Shah. Zafar Khan was originally a Hindu named Sādharan of the Tánk tribe (Khatri), and after his conversion to Islam became the head of the kitchen to Sultan Firoz Shah Tughlaq, who eventually appointed him Governor of Gujarat in place of the Farhat-ul-mulk. Muzaffar Shah was deposed by his son Tatarkhan with the aid of his uncle Shams Khan. Later, Shams Khan made common cause with Muzaffar Shah and poisoned Tatarkhan. On regaining his throne, Muzaffar Shah, to reward his services, gave Nagor as jagir to Shams Khan, where he and his descendants ruled for several generations, often paying tributes to Mewar or Marwar. Shams Khan was

---

1. Lane Pool's *Muhammadan Dynasties of India*, p. 313.

succeeded at Nagor by his son, Firoz Khan, who was a warrior of some renown. He measured swords with Kumbha's father, Maharana Mokal, who defeated him and destroyed his army at Jàwar, 20 miles south of Udaipur.[2] Firoz Khan had to return discomfited to Nagor.

The capture of Nagor in A.D. 1455 by Maharana Kumbha brought Sultan Qutbuddin of Ahmedabad into the field against him. With the King of Malwa, the Maharana had come into collision in the early part of his reign. These two kingdoms—the most powerful Mussalman principalities in India at the time—when defeated singly by the Maharana, combined and simultaneously invaded Mewar from the west and the south; but Kumbha, supported by the chivalry of Mewar and inspired by the patriotic valour of the Guhilot Rajputs, vanquished them both.

Sultan Qutbuddin died in A.D. 1458 and was succeeded by Dawud Shah. The kingdom of Gujarat continued to exist till Sultan Bahadur Shah was defeated by Humayun in A.D. 1535 and Gujarat annexed to the empire of Delhi. With Humayun's flight to Persia, Muhammad Shah Farukhi became Sultan of Gujarat but he and his successors were nominally rulers of Gujarat, till Akbar conquered it and made it a part of the Mughal Empire in A.D. 1584.

MALWA

Till about A.D. 1305, Malwa was ruled by the Hindus. In A.D. 1305, Ala-ud-din Khilji's army reduced Western Malwa

---

2. See Samiddheshwar Mahadeva Temple Inscription of *Magh Sud* 3rd, S. 1485 (A.D. 1429) at Chitor.

and soon after conquered Mandu. Malwa remained a province under the Sultans of Delhi till, in the reign of Sultan Mahmud II, the son of Firoz Shah Tughlaq, it became an independent monarchy in A.D. 1401. Firoz Shah Tughlaq (A.D. 1351–1388) had appointed Dilawar Khan Ghori, whose real name was Hassan, Governor of Malwa about A.D. 1373 Amir Timur captured Delhi on 18 December, A.D. 1398 and sacked it on the 28th. Sultan Mahmud Tughlaq, the son of Firoz Shah Tughlaq, fled towards Gujarat, and finding his way barred by Maharana Mokal, who inflicted a defeat on him at Raipur, he turned towards Malwa, where he was welcomed and royally entertained by Dilwar Khan. On Timur's departure, Mahmud Tughlaq returned to Delhi; and in A.D. 1401, Dilawar Khan proclaimed his independence and took up his residence at Dhar.

The kingdom of Malwa thus created, continued in existence till the year A.D. 1530 when Bahadur Shah of Gujarat conquered it and annexed it to his dominions. In A.D. 1570, Malwa became a part of the Mughal Empire when Baz Bahadur accepted Akbar's allegiance.

Dilawar Khan's reign was a very short one. He was murdered by his ambitious and unscrupulous son Alp Khan, who mounted the throne in A.D. 1405 under the title of Sultan Hoshang Ghori. He moved from Dhar to Mandu[3] and made it his capital in A.D. 1405. Sultan Hoshang Ghori's son and successor, Muhammad Ghazni Khan (A.D. 1434-36) was

---

3. *Journal of the Bombay Branch of the Royal Asiatic Society*, Special number LVIII, page 34.

murdered by his slave Mahmud Khan, who ascended the throne under the title of Sultan Mahmud Khilji and reigned from A.D. 1436 to A.D. 1475. During his reign, the kingdom of Malwa reached the zenith of its power and prosperity, and it was Sultan Mahmud Khilji that the Maharana challenged to stand the onslaught of the Rajputs. Sultan Mahmud Khilji was eventually defeated, caputred and imprisoned by the Maharana in the fort of Chitor.

The Maharana magnanimously set the Sultan free and resorted him to the throne of Mandu. His descendants ruled in Malwa till A.D. 1530, when Bahadur Shah of Gujarat defeated Sultan Mahmud Khilji II and annexed Malwa to Gujarat. Bahadur Shah, however, was defeated by Humayun, and Malwa and Gujarat both passed into Humayun's possession. But with the rise of Sher Shah, Humayun's power declined and one Malloo Khan, a slave of the old Khilji dynasty seized the throne of Malwa and began to reign in Mandu under the title of Sultan Qadir in A.D. 1534.

In A.D. 1543 Sher Shah drove away Malloo Khan and appointed Shuja Khan Governor of Malwa. Shuja Khan proclaimed his independence in A.D. 1553 and took up his residence in Sarangpur. On his death, his second son Baizeed murdered his elder brother and ascended the throne of Malwa under the title of Baz Bahadur. In A.D. 1564 Baz Bahadur accepted Akbar's allegiance and Malwa became a part of the Mughal Empire.

Six

Maharana's Conquest of Malwa and Capture of Sultan Mahmud Khilji

As Mahpa Panwar,[1] one of the assassins of Maharana Mokal, was given shelter by the Sultan of Mandu, a demand for his person was made by the Maharana. Sultan Mahmud Khilji, however, declined to surrender the refugee, pleading

---

1. His full name was Mahipal. His grandson Karamchand, Raja of Srinagar, gave shelter to Maharana Sangā, the grandson of Kumbhā during his days of adversity. See inscription of A.D. 1475 on the embankment of the lake at Pisangan, Ajmer District, described in the report of the Rajputana Museum, Ajmer for 1911-12. Mahipal's son Rughnath's queen Rajmati built the Pisangan lake and Karamchand's queen Ramadevi built the great lake at Ramsar in the province of Ajmer. The village Ramsar in olden days was a town of respectable size. It lies at a distance of 24 miles from Ajmer.

that it was against all notions of dignity and sovereignty to do so. The Maharana thereupon prepared for hostilities and left Chitor to attack Mandu. The Sultan advanced with a powerful army to meet the Maharana.

Rawat Chonda, the elder brother of Maharana Mokal, who had surrendered the throne of Mewar in favour of Mokal in circumstances which have made his name illustrious in the history of India, had taken up his residence in the court of Mandu, where the Sultan, Dilawar Khan Ghori, had received him with open arms and given him the district of Hallar as jagir for his maintenance. Sultan Mahmud Khilji now asked Chonda to lead the Mandu army against Rān Mal, the commander of the Mewar forces and take revenge for the murder of Rāghavadeva. The patriotic Chonda replied that he would gladly have led the army against Rān Mal's Rathods but that it was against his *dharma* to take up arms against the Maharana. Rather than stay at Mandu, he retired to his jagir.

The Maharana's army is said to have consisted of a hundred thousand horsemen and 1,400 elephants. The two armies met in A.D. 1437[2] near Sarangpur,[3] between Chitor and Mandsaur. After a severe engagement, the Sultan's army was utterly routed. The Kumbhalgarh Inscription, v. 270, says that Maharana Kumbha "captured countless Muslim women and burnt down Sarangpur."

---

2. Mahmud Khilji ascended the throne in A.D. 1436, and Rān Mal, who took a prominent part in this war was murdered in A.D. 1438. The Rānpur Temple Inscription of A.D. 1439 mentions the conquest of Mandor which followed Rān Mal's assassination.
3. The Rānpur Temple Inscription, lines 17–18, *Vide*, The Bhavanagar Inscriptions, page 114.

The Sultan fled and shut himself up in the fort of Mandu. The Maharana's army followed up the victory and laid siege to Mandu. When the Sultan was hard-pressed, he told Mahpa (Mahipal Panwar) that he could give him shelter no longer. Mahpa mounted his horse and going on to the rampart took a leap out of the fort. His horse was killed, but he was saved.[4] He fled to Gujarat. Kumbha stormed and took the fort. Rān Mal captured Sultan Mahmud Khilji, whose army fled in all directions. The Maharana returned to Chitor bringing the Sultan captive with him.

To commemorate this great victory, the Maharana built the great *Jaya Stambha*—Tower of Victory—in the fortress of Chitor, which still adorns that far-famed strong-hold, or as Colonel Tod says—"this ringlet on the brow of Chitor which makes her look down upon Meru with derision." Before, however, this *Tower of Victory*, a description of which is given in Chapter XIII, was completed, the Maharana had to face and vanquish the combination of the two most powerful kingdoms in India at the time, the Sultanates of Gujarat and Malwa, which glorious event is inscribed on the celebrated Tower.

Mahmud Khilji remained a prisoner[5] in Chitor for a period of six months, after which he was liberated without

---

4. *Vir Vinod*, Vol. I, p. 320.
5. *Vir Vinod*, p. 320. The place of imprisonment still exists. Beyond the palaces of Bhim and Padmini "within a stone enclosure, is the place where the victorious Kumbha confined the King of Malwa"— Archaeological Survey Reports, Vol. XXIII, p. 112.

ransom, by the magnanimous Maharana Kumbha.[6] "So far from showing any gratitude for the generosity thus shown him," says a historian of Mewar, he (the Sultan) spent the rest of his life in vain attempts at revenging himself on his conqueror, for which purpose he entered into an offensive alliance with his former foe, the Sultan of Gujarat."

Commenting on this victory, Colonel Tod[7] says:—"Abul Fazal relates this victory and dilates on Kumbha's greatness of soul in setting his enemy at liberty,[8] not only without ransom but with gifts. Such is the character of the Hindu; a mixture of arrogance, political blindness, pride and generosity. To spare a prostrate foe is the creed of the Hindu cavalier and he carries all such maxims to excess."

Political blindness and misplaced generosity on the part of Hindus so often illustrated in the history of India, has been the cause of their political downfall. They prided themselves on their chivalry which consisted of sparing foes, setting them at liberty after capturing them, and allowing them to return home unmolested. This no doubt proves that they were chivalrous and fearless, and lived on a high spiritual and moral plane; but it also proves that they were not men of foresight, and were, so far as politics go, novices and therefore unfit to preserve their liberties. The Rajput ideal of life was 'how to die nobly,' rather than how to achieve success

---

6. Tod's *Annals and Antiquities of Rajasthan*, Vol. I, p. 287. Also the *Gazetteer of Udaipur*, 1908, p. 17.
7. *Annals and Antiquities of Rajasthan*, Vol. I, p. 287.
8. As a matter of fact, Abul Fazal praised Sāngā for his capture and release of Sultan Mahmud Khilji II of Mandu.

in life. They preferred fame to success and cared less for victory and more for praise of their personal valour. The repeated attempts made by Sultan Mahmud Khilji of Malwa, after his release by the Maharana to wipe off his disgrace, by invading Mewar to obtain a victory over Maharana Kumbha, shows that Kumbha's release of Madmud Khilji was a piece of political folly, almost a crime. Had the Maharana destroyed the Sultanate of Malwa, annexed the country to Mewar and consolidated his kingdom as any wise ruler would have done he should not only have saved Mewar from the several wars with Malwa, which followed Mahmud Khilji's release, but would have spared Mewar the wars with the Sultans of Gujarat and the subsequent sack of Chitor by Bahadur Shah.

Several instances of such misplaced generosity may be cited. The Hun invader Mihirkula, who greatly oppressed the people of the Punjab, was defeated and taken prisoner about A.D. 131,[9] but was sent home with all honour by Bālāditya, the King of Magadha, with the result that Mihirkula invaded India again, treacherously murdered the King of Kashmir and seized his kingdom.[10]

Sultan Shahabuddin Ghori (Muizuddin-bin-Sam) was defeated and captured by Emperor Prithviraj Chauhan on the field of Tiraori in A.D. 1191 but was liberated and allowed to return to his country. He re-invaded India with an army of 1,20,000 horsemen and assisted by the Rajas of Kanauj and Anhilwara Patan, destroyed the Hindu Empire of India.

---

9. The *Krita Gupta Eras* in the *Modern Review* for July, 1932 p. 30.
10. Vincent Smith's *Early History of India*, p. 276.

Mahmud Khilji II, the King of Malwa was defeated and taken prisoner by Maharana Sānga in A.D. 1519. He was later not only set at liberty but was loaded with gifts and reinstated on his throne[11] by the chivalrous Maharana with the result that, soon after Sanga's death, this ungrateful man, to quote the Muslim historian Ferishta, "without any provocation, deputed Shiraj Khan with an army from Mandu to attack Maharana Ratan Singh,[12] son of Maharana Sanga."

Mehta Nainsi in his *Khyat*, page 69, relates how Maharana Pratap spared the life of the Commander-in-Chief of Akbar's army. In A.D. 1576, Akbar invaded Mewar and sent his Imperial legions under the supreme command of K. Man Singh of Jaipur. While Man Singh was bivouacing one evening at the village Lohsing with a thousand horsemen, ignorant of the fact that Maharana Pratap with his army was only two miles away behind the mountain, Maharana's scouts informed the Maharana of this god-sent opportunity to capture Man Singh. The Maharana could easily have wiped off Man Singh and the 1,000 horsemen, but out of chivalry not to take an enemy at unawares, Pratap abstained from attacking Man Singh and allowed him to escape.

Emperor Aurangzeb invaded Mewar in A.D. 1679. During the course of the war, he was hemmed in by the army of the Maharana and would, according to the English historian Orme, have perished in the mountain pass. He, however, owed his life to the clemency of Maharana Raj Singh who

---

11. Brigg's *Ferishta*, Vol. IV, p. 263.
12. *Ferishta*, Vol. IV, p. 266.

after confining the Emperor for two days, magnanimously ordered his army to withdraw from their stations and let Aurangzeb escape.[13] The Maharana's generosity did not stop here. When the Emperor was out of danger, the Maharana sent him his favourite Circassian wife, whom the Maharana had captured, accompanied by a chosen escort only requesting that the Emperor would in return refrain from destroying cows which might still be left in the plains. But for this act of foolish generosity, the whole history of India would have been changed and the country spared all the wars in the Deccan, in Rajputana and the Punjab, that filled the last thirty years of Aurangzeb's reign.

Well does Col. Tod exclaim:—"But for repeated instances of an ill-judged humanity, the throne of the Mughals might have been completely overturned."[14]

The time after Mahmud's defeat was very usefully employed by the Maharana in erecting several forts and generally strengthening the defences of his country.

---

13. Orme quoted in full in Tod's *Annals and Antiquities of Rajasthan*, Vol. I, p. 383, foot-note.
14. Tod's *Annals and Antiquities of Rajasthan*, Vol. I, p. 379.

Seven

Assassination of Rao Rān Mal and Maharana's Occupation of Marwar

After the crushing defeat and capture of the King of Malwa, Mahpá (Mahipal) Panwár and Ekká, son of Cháchá, fled to Gujarat. The Sultan of Gujarat, not risking the displeasure of the Maharana, being aware of the consequences to Malwa of giving shelter to the refugees, sent them away. Finding shelter nowhere, they came and threw themselves at the feet of the Maharana and sued for mercy. The Maharana, with his usual magnanimity, pardoned them and took them into his service. Rao Rān Mal disapproved of this clemency, but said nothing.[1]

The success which Rao Rān Mal had achieved in killing the assassins of Mokal, and crushing the power and capturing the person of the King of Malwa had raised the influence and

---

1. *Vir Vinod*, Vol I, p. 320–21.

power of the Rao to a pinnacle whence he exercised undisputed sway in Mewar. Rathods were to be seen everywhere in the kingdom, and all positions of confidence and trust as well as those of political and military importance, were bestowed on them. This naturally excited the apprehensions of the nobles and Sardars of Mewar. One day, Mahpá plainly told the Maharana that the Rathods were aiming at the throne of Mewar, but the Maharana, aware of his enmity towards Rao Rān Mal, gave no heed to this warning. Ekká, Cháchá's son, a few days later, while shampooing the Maharana, who was asleep, began to weep. His tears falling hot on the feet of the Maharana woke him, and on being asked the cause of his distress, he repeated the tale Mahpá had told.[2]

The Maharana now began to be a little suspicious of Rān Mal. The Maharana's *dhaya*[3] (wet nurse) became fearful of the future, and bursting with indignation at the ascendancy of the Rathods, demanded of the Rana's grandmother, "if her kin was to defraud her own grandchild of his inheritance."

The Dowager Queen Hansbai spoke to her brother. Rān Mal's reply did not allay her anxiety, which had been first caused by the assassination of Rághavadeva, the brother of Chondá. An incident which is said to have occurred about this time made the queen more anxious.

A fair maid of the Queenmother Sobhagyadevi, named Bhārmali, with whom Rao Rān Mal was in love, was one evening detained a little longer in the palace and went to him

---

2. *Vir Vinod*, Vol. I, p. 321; Nainsi's *Khyat*, p. 28.
3. The *dhaya* is an important person in a Rajput household.

later than usual. He asked the cause of the delay, whereupon she said that she was not her own mistress, and that as soon as those whose servant she was, gave her leave she went to him. The answer annoyed the Rao, who was drunk. He told her that she would soon cease to be a servant, and that those who cared to live in Chitor would have to live as her servants.[4] And, yielding to her seductive charms and female art, Rān Mal, intoxicated with liquor as he was, confessed to her his designs. The loyal maid, next day, related the whole incident to the Queen, who communicated the information to the Maharana. Whether this story of the maid Bharmali was concocted to sow seeds of dissension between the queenmother Sobhagyadevi, widow of Mokal and the Dowager Queen Hansbai, widow of Lakhsh Singh, or was invented as a part of the intrigue against Rān Mal, whose dominant position in Mewar had been the cause of the influx of Rathods in the country, it is impossible to believe that the chivalrous Rān Mal entertained the base designs attributed to him.

His high character, and his past conduct whether in Marwar or in Mewar, belie the imputations sought to be cast against him. His loyalty to the Maharana cannot be doubted. His position in the administration naturally excited the jealousy of the chiefs of Mewar. Whether some of them believed that Rān Mal's aim was to seize the supreme power in Mewar or not, they all thought that the time had come to rise against the Rathodisation of the Mewar administration

---

4. *Vir Vinod*, Vol. I, p. 321.

ASSASSINATION OF RAO RĀN MAL

and assert their right to hold important offices in their own country. There were two factions in Chitor, (*a*) the Sisodia nobles of Mewar and (*b*) the Rathods headed by Rān Mal. Rān Mal may have disclosed to Bharmali his intention to reduce the Sisodia nobility to a subordinate position and make the Rathod bureaucracy all powerful.

The Sisodia nobles of Mewar became apprehensive not only of their own position but of the future of their country. All their hopes for the safety of Mewar and its rightful sovereign now rested in Chondá; and to him they at once turned for help. He was apprised of the danger to his country and was asked to come and save it. Chondá, who had been a silent but not an inattentive spectator of the dangerous game that was being played in the land of his birth, lost no time in coming to the assistance of the Maharana.[5]

---

5. Various traditions are current in Mewar about Chonda's return to Chitor. One of them is to the effect that he sent 200 of his followers, hunters by profession, to visit their families in Chitor, and while there to ingratiate themselves in the favour of the gatekeepers of the fortress. The Maharana was asked to descend daily from the fort with a retinue to give feasts to the surrounding villages, and to hold the feast on the Diwali day at Ghosoonda. The day arrived: the feast was held at Ghosoonda, and night came, but no Chondá arrived. With heavy hearts, the *nurse*, the Purohit and others started homewards, and had reached the eminence called Chitori when forty horsemen passed them at full gallop, and at their head was the chivalrous Chondá, who, by a secret sign, paid homage to his nephew and sovereign. Chondá and his band reached the Rampol Gate unnoticed, but here they were challenged. They said they were neighbouring chieftains and had the honour to escort the Maharana home. But the main body, of

The *Vir Vinod* says[6] that the Rathods approached the queenmother Sobhagyadevi and in the interests of the Maharana, protested against Rawat Chondá's return to Chitor. The queen, however, replied that it did not look well that the gates of Chitor should be closed against one who had made such noble sacrifices for his country.

The old Rao of Mandor now began to scent danger. Fearing surprise, he sent his sons Jodhá (who later founded Jodhpur), Kándhal and others to live in the *taleti*, at the foot of the hill on which the fortress is built and told them to be always on their guard and never to come up to the fort even if they should receive a message in his name.[7] Prompted by Chondá, the Maharana asked Rān Mal to call Jodhá and Kándhal to reside in the fortress, but the Rao made some excuse or other.[8] The Sisodia nobles of Mewar now decided to rid the fortress of the Rathods.

Bhārmali, the queen's maid, one evening in *Asárh*, S. 1495 (A.D. 1438) plied the Rao with liquor. When the old chief was drunk, Bhārmali, who had been compelled to his embrace, tied him well to the bed with the big turban he wore. The

---

which this was the advance, presently coming up, the stratagem was discovered. Chondá unsheathed his sword, and at his well-known shout, the hunters were speedily in action. The Bhatti chief in charge of the principal post of Chitor, was killed, though not before he had launched his dagger at Chondá and wounded him.

6. *Vir Vinod*, Vol. I, p. 321.
7. Nainsi's *Khyat*, p. 28 (Benares Edition).
8. *Ibid.*

ASSASSINATION OF RAO RĀN MAL

Rao was only roused to a sense of his danger when Máhpá Panwár, Ekká son of Cháchá, and others arrived. In his rage, by a sudden desperate movement he got on his legs with the pallet behind him, and roared like a caged lion unable to free himself from the meshes of the turban that tied him to the pallet. Finding all arms removed, he got hold of a brass *lotá*, and with this he killed 3 of his 17 assailants ere he was killed by a shot from a matchlock.[9] Rān Mal was of herculean build. His gigantic stature and the force of his blow were well-known in Rajputana. Máhpá fled as soon as Rān Mal got on his feet. The other Rathods in the fortress, including Randhir, brother of Rān Mal, Sattā Bhati, son of Lunkaran, and Randhir Suráwat, were surprised and slain. Seeing the state of affairs a *Dom* in the service of Rān Mal, got on to the wall of the fortress and in a loud voice, cried out:—

चुंडा अजमल आविया, माढूं हुं धक आग।
जोधा रणमल मारिया, भाग सके तो भाग ॥

"Chondá has returned from Mandu. Rān Mal has been killed: Jodhá, flee for your life if you can."

Jodhá and his 700 Rathods saddled their horses, took up their arms and leaving Bheem, who was too drunk to move, sprang into their saddles and made for Marwar. Chondá, with the memory of the murder of his brother Rághavadeva fresh in his mind started in pursuit with ten thousand Guhilots. A

---

9. *Vir Vinod*, Vol. I, p. 322; Tod's *Rajasthan*, Vol. I, p. 280; Nainsi's Khyat (p. 28–29) gives a slightly different account.
The Jodhpur *Khyat* gives A.D. 1444, as the year of Rān Mal's murder.

running fight ensued between the Rathods and the Sisodias. There were several encounters.[10] Jodhá had not gone far when Chondá came up and a fight took place at Kapásan. Jodhá, after losing 200 men and killing 400 of the enemy, slipped away. Chardá and Chand Rao, sons of Aradakamal (Rān Mal's son), Rana Pitha Rájáwat, Sivaraj, Poorná Bháti, Barisál and others gave up their lives defending Jodhá.[11] Jodhá reached Mándal, where Kandhal joined him, and the two brothers continued their flight towards Marwar. They reached the Someshwar Pass in the hills which divide Marwar from Mewar with only a hundred horsemen. Chondá soon came up, and to prevent the Rathods escaping into Marwar made a furious attack on them. The Rathods collected round Jodhá and Kandhal to save them. Both the Sisodiás and the Rathods dismounted and engaged in a hand-to-hand fight. Out of the 100 horsemen that reached the Pass, Jodhá crossed it with but seven. With this remnant of the 700 horsemen with whom he had left Chitor, Jodhá set foot on the soil of Marwar. He owed his safety to the fleetness of his steed.

Chondá, who had patiently borne the wrongs heaped upon him by Rao Rān Mal, was exasperated beyond measure against the Rao and was determined to take full revenge for the ruin of his life wrought by Rān Mal, Chondá fully remembered that it was Rān Mal whose artful handling of the situation created by Chondá refusing the hand of Rān

---

10. The Jodhpur *Khyat* mentions encounters at Chitori, Satkhamba, Kanawaj, Kapasani and Kailwa.
11. Mehta Nainsi's *Khyat*, p. 29, also mentions Bhim, uncle of Jodhá as one of those who died defending Jodhá.

ASSASSINATION OF RAO RĀN MAL

Mal's sister Hansbai, had deprived him of the throne of Chitor. He also remembered that it was Rān Mal who had brought about his banishment from his motherland. He also remembered that his dear brother Rāghavadeva was murdered at the instance of Rān Mal. All these wrongs which had thoroughly embittered Chondá's life were raging within him life the fire which rages within an active valcano. And, now that the opportunity for which he had waited all his life, came, all the pent up fury and hatred burst out with a force which was almost uncontrollable.

Chondá's pursuit of Jodhá was relentless. He arrived at Mandawar (Mandor) close on Jodhá's heels. Jodhá unable to make a stand there, passed by it. Relying on the aid of the Bhátis of Poogal and Bikampur he took up his abode at the village Kāhuni,[12] ten miles from Bikaner.

The Rana's forces took possession of Marwar and established *thánás* all over the land. Akho Sisodia was appointed Governor of Mandor. Ahádo Hingolo and Mehta Rayangar were also attached to this fort. Ráwat Rághavadeva, son of Hansmal Chondawat, was given Sojat as jagir and was made Thánádar of Chokri. Bháti Banbir, Chauhán Jassá of Sachore and the son of Firoz Khan ruler of Nagor were also attached to this Tháná. *Vir Vinod* says that Chondá left his 3 sons Kuntal, Manja and Suwa at Mandor to keep the country under control.[13]

Narbad, son of Rān Mal's younger brother Sattá, to whom Maharana Mokal had given a jágir with an annual rental of

---

12. Marwar *Khyat*, Vol. I, p. 41.
13. *Vir Vinod*, Vol. I, p. 322.

Rs 1,00,000—Káyaláná—when Rān Mal was placed on the throne of Mandor in A.D. 1409, remained loyal throughout these transactions, and the Maharana enlarged his jagir by further bestowing on him an estate yielding an income of Rs. 50,000 a year. He took up his abode at Bassi. The year A.D. 1438 thus saw the expulsion of the Rathods from Chitor and the passing of Marwar into the possession of the Maharana.[6]

---

6. The Rānpur Temple Inscription of A.D. 1439 mentions the occupation of Mandor by Maharana Kumbha.

Eight

Rao Jodhá Recovers Marwar

After a year's stay at Kahuni, Jodhá began to raid Mandor. His raids always cost him men and horses without bringing him any profit. One day, returning from his raid, Jodhá came to a village and put up at the house of one Rákan Jat. The mistress of the house placed before Jodhá a *tháli* (plate) full of hot *ghát* (porridge). Jodhá at once thrust his fingers into the centre of the porridge to take a morsel, and as the porridge was burning hot, Jodhá burnt his fingers. Seeing this and not knowing who the stranger was, the Játni said: "Brother, thou art as devoid of sense as Jodhá is." Jodhá was astonished to hear this remark and asked the lady why she thought Jodhá was without sense. The Jatni replied that want of sense in Jodhá was clear from the fact that instead of raiding the out-lying country, he always went straight to attack Mandor, which was garrisoned by the Rana; and thus at every encounter he lost horses and men without gaining his object. And thou, too, my brother, added the lady, lacketh sense inasmuch as thou putteth thy hand straight into the centre of the porridge and burneth thy fingers. If thou wouldst but begin with the porridge near the edge which is not so hot, thou shouldst have by and by the porridge in the centre of the plate too, as it is not going to run away.[1]

Jodhá took this advice to heart and gave up going towards Mandor and began to raid the country around. This brought him plunder, and he got around him a body of horsemen. His brothers also grew up and began to assist him. With the help of the Bhátis of Kelhan, where he had married, he began to raise disturbances in the country. He was, however, seriously handicapped by want of horses and lack of money. There was famine, too, in the land and grain was scarce.

While Jodhá was thus roaming homeless in Marwar, his country being in the Maharana's possession, an incident occurred which roused him and put fresh energy into his activities.

The Dowager Queen of Mewar, Rao Rán Mal's sister, sympathising with Jodhá in his forlorn state, one day begged the Maharana to restore Mandor to the young Rao, telling him how Rán Mal had come to Chitor to help the Maharana at a critical time, slain Cháchá and Mairá, defeated the Mussalmans, raised the credit of Mewar, and was killed there, and that his son Jodhá was now wandering in the jungles, homeless and hopeless. Such, said the lady, was the reward for services rendered to Mewar. The Maharana replied that

---

1. Marwar *Khyat*, Vol. I, pp. 41–42.

Rān Mal had murdered Rághavadeva, Chondá's brother, which Chondá could never forget, and that he, for fear of wounding Chondá's feelings, could not do anything to help Jodhá, but promised that if Jodhá should take Mandor he would not molest him. Thus assured, the old lady sent a confidential messenger, a *Cháran* named Dulá, to Jodhá to communicate to him the views of the Maharana and to encourage him to make an effort and take Mandor.

Cháran Asiá Dulá went in search of Jodhá, and eventually reaching the village Bhádang, in the jungles of Padává, in the sandy desert of Marwar, he found him with his fifty horsemen and some foot followers in the act of satisfying their hunger with the *bájri* growing in the fields. The message from Hansbai, the Dowager Queen of Mewar,[2] acted like a powrful tonic on him, and he set about collecting means to effect his purpose. He went straight to Ráwat Lunkaran of Satráwa, who had got 500 horses in his stables, and appealed to his patriotism, and reminded him of his duty to his kindred and asked for 200 horses. Lunkaran declined to give the horses, saying that he held his fief from the Maharana, who would deprive him of the land if he should give him assistance. Disappointed by the Ráwat, Jodhá went to the Thakuráni, who was a sister of Jodhá's mother. She was a Bhatyáni lady, a class well-known amongst the Rajputs for wisdom and foresight. Seeing Jodhá dejected, she enquired the cause. He told her that the Ráwat had refused him horses of which he was in sore need. The Bhatyáni asked him to cheer up, saying

---

2. *Vir Vinod*, Vol, I, p. 324.

the horses were all his. She sent for the Ráwat and asked him to put certain valuables in the *Tosháhkáná*; and when he unlocked the room and went in to deposit the things, the Thakuráni promptly shut the door and locked him in. She then sent one of her maids with Jodhá to the stables with the message that the Ráwat had ordered that the stables were at Jodhá's disposal, and that the keepers were fully to equip any horses that he wished to take away. Jodhá picked out 140 of the best steeds of Satráwá, mounted his Rajputs and marched away. When he was gone the Thakuráni unlocked the door of the Tosháhkáná. Ráwat Lunkaran came out boiling with rage, quarrelled with the Thakuráni, scolded his Kámdárs and had the keepers of the stables beaten, but could not get back the horses.[3]

Jodhá thus equipped went to enlist the support of Harbá Sánkhlá, the celebrated cavalier of Rajputana, whose deeds of chivalry are sung everywhere in the country. This great man, a *Bála Brahmachári* (he who leads a life of celibacy from childhood), lived a life of simplicity and asceticism, and was ever ready to succour the distressed, help the weak and champion the cause of the oppressed. His generosity was proverbial, his door was open to all who sought his aid, his lance ever ready to go to the assistance of a suppliant with a just grievance. His house, a place of shelter to all who went there, provided unbounded hospitality to the stranger. He had

---

3. The following couplet refers to the incident:—
   ज्यूं ज्यूं कहियो रावत लूणो ।
   त्यूं त्यूं लड़े घणेरो सूणो ॥

been performing the rite of *Sadāvrat*, at which everyone is shown hospitality and granted his request. Jodhá, with a hundred and twenty followers, arrived when the 'stranger's fare' had been distributed. Harbá had a hurried meal of *mujd* boiled with flour, sugar and spices prepared and set before the Rao and his followers, who enjoyed the pottage and went to sleep.

On waking, they stared at one another, for their moustachios were dyed with the evening's meal. Harbá, however, remarked "that the grey of age was thus metamorphosed into the tint of morn and hope, so would their fortunes become young and Mandor again be theirs."

Thus aided, Jodhá started to recover his patrimony. He first attacked the Maharana's *thána* of Chaukri. Rághavadeva Rathod with his small following fled, leaving everything behind, and Bháti Randir, Rana Visaldeva, Ráwal Duda of the Rana's officers were killed. Jodhá next attacked and took Kosáná, and by rapid marches arrived at Mandor. Two sons of Rawat Chondá, Kándhal and Manjá, were in charge of the place. Despising the numbers of the enemy, and ignorant of the fact that the assailants included Harbá Sánkhlá, they descended sword in hand to meet them. But they were overpowered; Kándhal was slain and Manjá took to his horse and fled but was pursued, overtaken and slain on the way. Ahádo Hingolo, Sisodiá Eko and others were also slain. A *chhatri* still marks the place on the Balsamad Lake, near Jodhpur, where Hingolo fell after performing deeds of valour, Chauhán Jassá, Harbhám Sindhal, Visaldeva Parmar and the son of Firoz Khan of Nagor fled. Jodhá recovered Mandor. In a few days, Jheá also seized Sojat and took up his abode there. Chondá would have invaded Marwar to take *vair* (revenge)—as two sons of his had fallen while Mandor had lost only one chief, Rān Mal—but abstained on learning that the Maharana forbade it. Conscious, however, of the superior power of Mewar, Jodhá made peace with the Maharana. We find that Jodhá's daughter, Sringardevi, was married to Maharana Kumbha's son Raimal.[4] The inscription in the *baodi* (stepped well) built by Sringardevi in A.D. 1504 in Ghosundi, 12 miles from Chitor, describes her as Rao Jodhá's daughter and wife of prince Raimal.

Thus after 7 years, occupation[5] of it by the Maharana, Jodhá won back Mandor by the sword about A.D. 1445.

---

4. Bengal Asiatic Society's Journal, Vol. 55, Part I, pp. 79–82.
5. The following verse supports the fact that the Maharana occupied Marwar for seven years:—

थाणो जाय मंडावर थट्यो जोरकर लखपत
कियो राज चूंडे नव कोटा सात बरस ताईं सीसोद

"Lakhpat (Maharana) established a thana (military post) at Mandor; Chondá Sisodia ruled Marwar (Nava Kota) for seven years." See *Vir Vinod*, Vol. I, p. 324.

Nine

Conquest of Abu and Haravati

The kingdom of Sirohi lies in the south-west part of Rajputana, between 24',20" and 25'.17" latitude and 72'.16" and 73'.10" longitude, and is 1,964 miles in area. Its rulers belong to the Deora branch of the Chauhan Rajputs. The most important place in this kingdom is Mount Abu, the highest point of the Aravalli Hills (Adāvalā) stretching from Delhi to Gujarat. Mount Abu, the 'Olympus of the Hindus' as Colonel Tod calls it, was the seat of a powerful kingdom in old days. Abu formed part of the empire of Emperor Chandragupta of the Mauriya dynasty, who ruled early in the fourth century B.C. The territory of Abu passed successively into the possession of the Khshtrapas, the Imperial Guptas, the Vaisa dynasty of which Emperor Sri Harsha was the ornament; Chaoras, the Solankis, and the Parmārs. From the Parmārs, the Chauhans of Jalor took the kingdom of Abu. Lumba, a scion of the younger branch of the Chauhan rulers of Jalor, seized Abu from the Parmar Raja Hoon about the year A.D. 1311 and became the first king of the territory now known as the kingdom of Sirohi. The famous town of Chandravati, situated about four miles to the south of the present Abu Road Railway station on the B.B. & C.I. Ry. Was then the capital of the kingdom, and Lumba took up his residence there and ruled till A.D.1320. Maharao Sahas Mal, the seventh in descent from Lumba,[1] finally abandoned Chandravati, founded the present town of Sirohi[2] and made it the capital of his kingdom in A.D. 1425.

Sahas Mal was an ambitious ruler and made attempts to extend his dominions on all sides. He found his opportunity in the civil turmoil that followed the assassination of Maharana Mokal. He annexed some of the territory ruled by the Solanki Rajputs lying nearby, and finding Maharana Kumbhakaran engaged in punishing his father's murderers began to encroach on the Maharana's territory and took possession of a few villages on the borders of Mewar. When the Maharana came to know of this aggression he was not slow to take action. As soon as the rebels were disposed of, Maharana Kumbha sent an expedition against Maharao Sahas Mal under Dodiya Narsingh son of Rao Shalji. Narsingh captured the strong-hold of Abu, seized Basantgarh and Bhula

---

1. Sahasmal was son of Shiv Bhan, who was son of Rān Mal; Rān Mal was son of Salkha, who was son of Samant Singh: Samant Singh was son of Kānhad Deva, who was son of Tej Singh; Tej Singh; Tej Singh was son of Lumba.
2. Mahamahopadhyaya P. Gauri Shankar's *History of Sirohi*, page 194.

CONQUEST OF ABU AND HARAVATI   61

and annexed[3] the whole of the eastern part of the Sirohi territory to Mewar. A copper plate inscription of A.D. 1437 *Asar*, V.S. 1494) found in the Nandiya village and at present deposited in the Rajputana Museum, Ajmer mentioning a grant of land in village *Chavarli* in the Ajari *pargannah* of Sirohi, shows that that part of the Sirohi territory had passed into the Maharana's possession before the year A.D. 1437.

The Sirohi *Khyat* says that Maharana Kumbha was allowed by Maharao Lakha of Sirohi to retire to Abu when attached by the Sultan of Gujarat, that the Maharana refused to give up Abu after the Sultan's army returned to Ahmedabad, and that Lakha thereupon attacked the Maharana and recovered Abu from him. This can not be true, for there is incontestable evidence that the Maharana had taken possession of Abu before A.D. 1437, while Maharao Lakha came to the throne of Sirohi only in A.D. 1451.[4] It also appears from *Mirati Sikandari*, that the Maharana was in possession of Abu in A.D. 1456 and that Abu had been taken by Kumbha by force of arms from Sirohi. The *Mirati Sikandari* says that when Sultan Qutbuddin of Gujarat invaded the Maharana's dominions in A.D. 1456 in order to avenge his defeat at Nagor by Maharana Kumbha, the Maharao of Sirohi met the Sultan on the way and offered him his services and requested him to wrest the fort of Abu from the Maharana and restore it to the Maharao, as it was the hereditary seat of the Rajas of Sirohi, and the Maharana had *forcibly deprived*

---

3. History of Sirohi by Mahamahopadhyaya P. Gauri Shanker Ojha, p. 194. Also, his *History of Udaipur*, Vol. I, p. 283.
4. Gauri Shanker Ojha's *History of Sirohi*, p. 197.

the Maharo of it. The Sultan detached an army under Malik Shaaban Imadul Mulk to attack Abu, conquer it and restore it to Sirohi. Imadul Mulk had to pass through narrow passes, and the Rajputs from the heights attacked the Gujarat forces from all sides, and defeated the Malik, inflicting severe losses.

The Chitor *Tower of Victory Inscription*, verse 284, says:—"The great Maharana by force of arms, conquered Abu and built the fort of Achalgarh on the summit of the hill, and as an offering to Vishnu, built the temple of Kumbhaswami there. The *Ekling-Mahatamya*, written in Kumbha's time, says the same thing. The song which ends with the couplet:—

डोडे राव सिरोही दुजडा दलसजड़ा पर हंस दिया।
आबु गिरवर शिखर ऊपरां कुम्भे सरवर महल किया ॥

celebrates this event. The couplet says that Kumbha after conquering Abu, constructed a lake and a palace there.[5]

CONQUEST OF BUNDI

Bundi is now the head of the ruling houses of the great Chauhan family of the Rajputs. The Chauhans reached the zenith of their prosperity and greatness when Prithviraj, King of Ajmer ruled the whole of Northern India as its last Hindu Emperor (A.D. 1179 to 1191) Ater the death of Prithviraj, the Chauhans declined rapidly. Prithviraj's son Govindraj was driven out of Ajmer by Prithviraj's younger brother Hariraj

---

5. See *Vir Vinod*, Vol. I, p. 332.

for accepting Shahbuddin Ghori's suzereinty,[6] and had to retire to the famous fortress of Ranthambhor. He and his descendants ruled there for several generations. The last representative of this House, the celebrated King Hammira was killed fighting against Sultan Allauddin Khilji of Delhi[7] in A.D. 1301 and the rule of the direct descendants of Prithviraj came to an end in Rajputana.

Another branch of the Chauhan family headed by Luxman, the younger brother of King Sinhraj of Ajmer, took possession of Nadole and founded a kingdom there in V.S. 1024 (A.D. 967).[8] The seventh in descent from him, Alhan (V.S. 1209–218=A.D. 1152–1161) was reigning at Nadole, when his younger brother Manikraj migrated to Bambaoda in Mewar. One of his descendants, Har Raj called Hārā, gave the name Hara to the family which is now known as the Hārā Rajputs, and their country as Haravati. Har Raj's grandson Deoraj took Bundi[9] in V.S. 1398=A.D. 1341 from its Mina rulers with the assistance of Maharana Ari Singh[10] and founded the kingdom of Bundi. Its rulers always recognised the Maharana of Mewar as their overlords.

During the confusion following the murder of Mokal and the rebellion of Chachá and Mairá, the Hāras of Bundi threw off their allegiance to Mewar and took possession of the fort

---

6. *Ajmer: Historical and Descriptive*, p. 156.
7. *Hammira of Ranthambhor*, p. 46.
8. Gaurishanker Ojha's *History of Sirohi*, p. 166.
9. Tod's *Rajasthan*, Vol. II, p. 460.
10. Nainsi's *Khyat*, Vol. I, pp. 105–6.

of Amargarh by a stratagem, and began to molest the Rajputs of Mandlgarh.

Maharana Kumbha, therefore, invaded Haravati, took Amargarh where a large number of the Hārās including Toghji, the governor of the fort, were killed. He also conquered Bambaoda, Bundi, Khatgarh and Mandalgarh[11] and reduced the Hārās to submission. The Kumbhalgarh Inscription, verse 265, states that the Maharana "vanquished the Hārās and received a tribute from them."

The Maharao of Bundi sued for pardon and was allowed to retain Bundi on payment of the expenses of the invasion and a fine. The conquest of Bundi is mentioned in the Ranpur Temple Inscription of A.D. 1439 (V.S. 1496) and must therefore, have taken place in that year or sometime before it. Thus, the two chief Chauhan ruling families of his time, who had dared to encroach on the Mewar territory, the one in the west and the other in the east, were defeated and the greater part of their territories annxed to Mewar by Maharana Kumbha.

---

11. The Kumbhalgarh Inscription of A.D. 1460.

Ten

Wars with the Sultans of Malwa and Gujarat

We now turn to the foreign relations of Mewar and see how the valiant Maharana not only successfully defended his country against the attacks, first made singly and when thus defeated, made in combination by the Kings of Malwa and Gujarat, then at the zenith of their power and prestige, but carried the war into the countries of his foes, humbled their pride, took from them several forts and cities, extended his dominions on all sides and became the most powerful sovereign of his time in India.

In A.D. 1443, Maharana Kumbha had to go to Haravati to punish some rebels. Finding Mewar unprotected, Sultan Mahmud Khilji of Mandu, who had been smarting under the shame of having been kept a prisoner in Chitor by Maharana Kumbha, and burning with a desire to take revenge and wipe off his disgrace of A.D. 1437, invaded Mewar. Arriving near Kumbhalgarh, he prepared to destroy the temple of Bān Mata in the village Kailwara, at the foot of the hill. This big temple had a fortified wall round it and contained some munitions of war. Despairing of making any impression on the fort of Kumbhalgarh, the Sultan determined to use all his resources to seize this temple and himself led the assault on it. The Maharana's Sardar, Thakur Dip Singh, who lived in it, collected his warriors and opposed the Sultan. For seven days, Dip Singh successfully repulsed all attempts of the Sultan's army to take possession of the temple. On the seventh day, Dip Singh was killed and the temple fell into the hands of the Sultan. He razed it to the ground, burnt the stone image of the Nundi (bull) found in it and used the lime with betel leaves. Flushed with this small success, he started for Chitor, and leaving a part of his army to take the fortress, advanced to attack the Maharana, sending his father, Azam Humayun, towards Mandsaur to lay waste the Maharana's country.

When the Maharana heard of these events, he left Haravati to return to his dominions and came upon the Sultan's army near Mandalgarh. A battle was fought here in which the Sultan was defeated, but the defeat was not decisive.[1] A few days later the Maharana made a night attack

---

1. Ferishta (Vol. IV, page 210) says that the Maharana attacked the Sultan on 26th April A.D. 1443 with an army of 12 thousand horse and 6,000 infantry but was unsuccessful. The next day, the Sultan obtained some loot and returned to Mandu with the intention of attacking Chitor the following year. The historians of Rajputana say that the Sultan was defeated but the defeat was not decisive.

WARS WITH THE SULTANS OF MALWA AND GUJARAT 67

on the Sultan who was utterly defeated and fled towards Mandu.[2] Ferishta says: "The Sultan returned without molestation to Mandu."— Vol. IV, p. 210. This is Ferishta's way of describing a defeat.

To retrieve this fresh disaster, Mahmud set about preparing another army, and four years later, on 20th Rajab, H. 850 (*Kartik Bad* 6th, S. 1503), 11 October A.D. 1446, he went towards Mandalgarh with a large army. Reaching Rampura (now in Indore State) he appointed Malik Saifuddin as governor there in place of Bahadur and moved further. The Maharana's army attacked him while he was crossing the river Banas,[3] and having defeated him, drove him back to Mandu. For about 10 years after this defeat, Mahmud Khilji did not venture to take the offensive against the Maharana.

Ferishta, in conformity with the practice of Persian historians, who ignore or try to whitewash defeats and unfavourable issues, says (Vol. IV, p. 210) that the Sultan returned after taking Nazrana. This is obviously far from true. For, had the Sultan obtained a victory and concluded peace after receiving Nazrana, why should be have, as stated by Ferishta himself (Vol. IV, p. 215) sent Taj Khan with eight thousand cavalry and 20 elephants to attack Chitor without any cause whatever from Bayana, where he had gone immediately after his return to Mandu. Had the Sultan achieved a victory, we should not have found him (as will be seen later) asking the King of Gujarat for help, and proposing

---

2. *Vir Vinod* of Mahamahopadhyaya Kaviraj Shamaldas Vol. I, p. 325.
3. *Vir Vinod*, Vol. I, page 325.

to him when that Sultan too had been defeated by the Maharana, an offensive alliance against the Maharana.

In A.D. 1454, however, Sultan Mahmud Khilji made another attempt to attack Chitor, but the Maharana attacked him before he came near Chitor and inflicted a severe defeat on him which compelled him to return to Mandu. Ferishta says (Vol. IV, page 222) that the Sultan sent Prince Gayasuddin to take Ranthambhor and himself started to attack Chitor, and that leaving Mansur-ul-Mulk to lay waste the district of Mandsaur, himself advanced and threatened to appoint his own governor there and found a town and named it Khiljipur. Thereupon, the Maharana tendered submission, and the Sultan seeing the approach of the rainy weather, returned to Mandu with some gold. Instead of saying that the Sultan returned discomfited and defeated, Ferishta puts it nicely and says that Sultan owing to the approach of the rains returned after taking some gold!

About this time (A.D. 1454) the state of affairs at Ajmer drew the Sultan's attention to it. This important city—'the heart of Rajputana'—is a place of the greatest strategical importance in Upper India. It stands at the summit of the plateau which marks the highest elevation on the plains of Hindustan. Its political importance is proved by the fact that every power aspiring to dominate the country has first taken possession of it and used it as a ladder to mount to political supremacy in India. Its religious importance is due to the existence of Pushkar, the King of Hindu places of pilgrimage in its environs, and the mausoleum of Khwaja Muinuddin Chishti in the town. The death of Swami Dayanand Saraswati

WARS WITH THE SULTANS OF MALWA AND GUJARAT

at Ajmer, invests the place with peculiar importance in the eyes of Reformed Hinduism.[4]

During the reign of Maharana Mokal, Rao Rān Mal of Mandor had wrested this strong-hold from the Sultans of Delhi and restored it to Mewar. Acting on the advice of *pancholi* Khemsi, Rān Mal sent him with a picked force of Rathods to take Ajmer. Under the pretence of conveying a daughter to the Viceroy of Ajmer, he introduced his men into that renowned fortress, the ancient strong-hold of the Chauháns, putting the Delhi garrison to the sword. Salim Shah, the King of Multan, who had gone on pilgrimage to Ajmer after killing Chondá, father of Rao Rān Mal at Nagor was also killed by the Rajputs. Khemsi was rewarded with the grant of the township of Khatoo, then lately captured from the Káimkhanees.[5]

In A.D. 1454, Mahmud Khilji having received representations that all Muhammadan religious practices had been forbidden in Ajmer[6] by the Hindu governor of the place, and receiving promises of help from its Mussalman residents, undertook an expedition against that city. Ajmer was in the possession of the Maharana and the Sultan did not venture openly to invade it. He had recourse to a *ruse*. Sending the bulk of his army against Mandsaur to keep the Maharana's forces engaged, he advanced and attacked Ajmer. Gajádhar Singh, the governor of the fort of Ajmer, defended the fort for four days, and then, despising the foe's forces, he came out and attacked the Sultan's army. He was killed after

---

4. See my "Ajmer: Historical and Descriptive" p. 23.
5. The Jodhpur *Khyat*.
6. Brigg's *Ferishta*, Vol. IV, page 222.

performing deeds of valour and slaying numbers of the enemy. As his men were retiring into the fort, the Sultan's men mixed themselves among the Rajputs and entered it. The Sultan thus obtained possession of the fort but 'not without sustaining severe loss.'[7] He appointed Khwaja Naimatullah as governor of the fort, with the title of Saif Khan, and himself went towards Mandalgarh.

As he approached the river Banas, the Maharana's army came out of the fort and fell upon the Sultan, who sustained a severe defeat and fled to Mandu.

Ferishta says: "Rana Kumbha, at the head of a body of Rajputs, attacked one flank of the king's army under Taj Khan and sent another body to attack that under Ali Khan. A severe engagement ensued in consequence, when the retreat was mutually sounded. On the following morning, the Malwa officers persuaded the Sultan of the necessity of his army retiring into quarters, both on account of the reduced numbers and the wretched state of the camp equipment, now rendered almost useless, which circumstances, together with the approach of the rainy season, induced Sultan Mahmud to return to Mandu."—Brigg's English translation of *Ferishta*, Vol. IV, p. 223. Briggs in a foot-note says: "The *drawn battle* mentioned by the Malwa historians must be deemed a *defeat*."

An attack on Mandalgarh made by the Sultan[8] in A.D. 1456 also failed and the Sultan had to return to Mandu

---

7. *Ferishta*, Vol. IV, page 222.
8. *Ferishta* says that the Sultan failed to take the fort itself but after 11 months' seige was able to take the lower fort and, then retired to Mandu after receiving some money,—Brigg's *Ferishta*, Vol. IV, p. 223.

WARS WITH THE SULTANS OF MALWA AND GUJARAT

discomfited. Altogether, five attempts were made by the Sultan to wipe out his disgrace of A.D. 1437, but every time he was defeated by the Maharana.

Sultan Mahmud Khilji, now convinced that it was impossible to cope with Maharana Kumbha single-handed, resolved to ask the Sultan of Gujarat to combine with him and, thus united, attack the Maharana. For this purpose, he sent his prime minister Taj Khan to Gujarat.

About this time, Sultan Mahmud Khilji's son Prince Umar Khan, owing to disagreement with his father fled to Ahmedabad, but finding no support there came to Maharana Kumbha, who gave him shelter and kept him in Chitor for a long time. Later, he was killed in an encounter with the Sultan at Chanderi.[9]

The same year (Hijra 860=A.D. 1454) Firoz Khan, Khan of Nagor, died.[10] He belonged to the family of the Sultan's of Gujarat. His father Shams Khan had obtained from his elder brother Muzaffar Shah, the first Sultan of Gujarat, the province of Nagor. On Firoz Khan's death, his elder son, Shams Khan so named after his grandfather, succeeded him, but Firoz Khan's younger brother, Mujahid Khan, deposed him and prepared to take his life. Shams Khan fled to Maharana Kumbha for shelter and help.[11] Kumbhá, who had long had designs on Nagor, gladly embraced this opportunity of carrying them out, and agreed to place Shams Khan on the throne of Nagor on the condition that he acknowledged

---

9. *Vir Vinod*, Vol. I, page 327.
10. *Ferishta*, Vol. IV, p. 40 (Cal. Edition of 1910).
11. Bayley's *Gujarat*, page 148.

Maharana Kumbha's supremacy by demolishing a part of the battlements of the fort of that place.[12] Shams Khan accepted the terms.[13] The Maharana marched with a large army to Nagor, defeated Mujahidkhan, who fled towards Gujarat, and placed Shams Khan on the *gádi* of Nagor, and demanded of him the fulfilment of the condition. As preparations were being made for the demolition of the battlements, one of the old Pathan officers of Shams Khan cried out: "Would that Firoz had a daughter instead of a son, for even she would not have allowed her father to be disgraced by permitting the dismantling of the fortifications of the fort."[14] On this, Shams Khan humbly prayed to the Maharana to spare the fort just then, for otherwise his nobles would kill him after the Maharana was gone. He promised to demolish the battlements himself later on. The Maharana granted this prayer and returned to Mewar.

No sooner, however, had Kumbhá reached Kumbhalgarh than Shams Khan, instead of demolishing, began to strengthen the fortifications of Nagor. This brought Maharana Kumbha on the scene again with a large army. Shams Khan was driven out of Nagor, which passed into Kumbhá's possession. The Maharana now demolished the fortifications of Nagor, thus carrying out his long-cherished design. The Maharana took away from the treasury of Shams

---

12. *Ferishta*, Vol. IV, page 40, Also Bayley's *History of Gujarat*, page 148, foot-note.
13. *Ferishta*, Vol. IV, page 41.
14. Bayley's *History of Gujarat*, page 148, foot-note.

WARS WITH THE SULTANS OF MALWA AND GUJARAT 73

Khan a large store of precious stones, jewels and other valuable things. The *Eklinga Mahatmya* composed during Kumbhá's lifetime, says that he "defeated the King of the Shakas (Mussalmans), put to flight Mashiti (Mujahid Khan), slew the heroes of Nágpur (Nagor), destroyed the fort, filled up the moat round the fort, captured elephants, imprisoned large number of Shak (Muslim) women and punished countless Mussalmans. He gained a victory over the King of Gujarat, burnt the city[15] (Nagor) with all the mosques therein, liberated twelve lakhs of cows from the Muslims, made the land a pasture for cows and gave Nagor for a time to Bráhmans."[16] He carried away the gates of the fort, and an image of Hanumán from Nagor, which he fixed to the principal gate of the fortress of Kumbhalgarh, calling it the Hanumán Pol.[17]

The Chitrogarh *Kirtisthambha* Inscription repeats these facts, and says that he destroyed "the great mosque built by Sultan Firoz, which showed Muslims the way to Nagor", (verse 19) and dismantled the fort and filled up the moat. "He uprooted the Mussalman tree of Nagor and destroyed it with all its mosques," Verse 22; and took away Shams Khan's treasure containing heaps of jewels (V. 23).

---

15. Kumbha's commentary on the *Gita Govinda*, verses 60–62, also reiterates these things.
16. *See* also Chitorgarh *Kirtisthambha* Inscription.
17. *Vir Vinod* Vol. I, p. 352, says the Maharana carried away the image of Hanuman from Nagor. The Kumbhalgarh Inscription, however, says that the image had been brought by Kumbha from Mandor.

Shams Khan fled to Ahmedabad, taking with him his daughter, whom he gave to Sultan Qutb-ud-din to wife.[18] The Sultan thereupon espoused his cause and sent a large army under Rái Rám Chandar and Malik Gadday to take back Nagor. The Maharana allowed the army to approach Nagor, when he came out, and after a severe engagement inflicted a crushing defeat on the Gujarat army, annihilating it. Only remnants of it reached Ahmedabad, to carry the news of the disaster to the Sultan.[19]

Sultan Qutb-ud-din now took the field in person, determined to wrest Nagor back from the Maharana. The Maharana advanced to meet him and came to Mount Abu.

When the Sultan after leaving Ahmedabad came near Abu, the Maharao of Sirohi went to him and asked him to restore Abu to him, which the Maharana had wrested from him. The Sultan sent his Commander-in-Chief, Malik Shaaban Imad-ul-Mulk, with a large army, to take the fort of Abu from the Maharana, and himself proceeded towards the fortress of Kumbhalgarh.[20] Kumbhá, aware of this plan, came out, attacked and "defeated Imad-ul-Mulk with great slaughter,"[21]

---

18. Bayley's *Gujarat*, page 149; *Ferishta*, Vol. IV, page 41.
19. *Bombay Gazetteer*, page 242, *Ferishta*, Vol. IV, page 41.
20. Ferishta says that the Sultan "despairing of reducing Chitor" went towards Abu,—Vol. IV, p. 41.
21. *Bombay Gazetteer*, Vol. I, page 242. Also Bayley's History of Gujarat, page 149. The *Mirati Sikandari* states that the enemy poured down on him on all sides and he was defeated with loss of many men. Ferishta, however, states that the Raja of Sirohi, who was a relation of the Maharana met the Sultan in battle but was defeated, and that the Sultan then went away towards Kumbhalgarh. *Tarikhi Alfi* says that Shaaban after suffering heavy losses, was recalled.

WARS WITH THE SULTANS OF MALWA AND GUJARAT

and by forced marches reached Kumbhalgarh before the Sultan arrived there.

Imad-ul-Mulk returned discomfited to the Sultan, and both arrived at the foot of the hill on which is perched the fortress of Kumbhalgarh. The Maharana sallied out of the fortress and attacked and defeated the Sultan, who sustained a heavy loss, and losing all hope of taking this strong-hold, retired to Gujarat.[22]

The Kings of Malwa and Gujarat, thus completely defeated by the Maharana one after another, now resolved to combine and invade Mewar. As stated before, Sultan Mahmud Khilji of Malwa had become convinced that singlehanded he could never succeed against the Maharana and had resolved, to form an alliance with the Sultan of Gujarat. He, therefore, sent his *Vazir*, Taj Khan, to Ahmedabad. As Sultan Qutb-ud-din of Gujarat was returning discomfited, after his defeat at the Maharana's hands, to Ahmedabad, Taj Khan met him on the way and proposed a formal offensive alliance against the Maharana, who had destroyed the Mussalman Chiefship of Nagor and had defeated them both. The King of Gujarat eagerly listened to the proposal and accepted the terms of the alliance, which was ratified at Chānpāner by Sheikh Nizam-ud-din and Malik-ul-Ulema on behalf of Sultan Mahmud Khilji, and by Qazi Hisam-ud-din on behalf of Sultan Qutb-ud-din, towards the close of the year A.D. 1456.[23] It was agreed between the two kings that the southern part

---

22. The *Bombay Gazetteer*, page 242.
23. Brigg's *Ferishta*, Vol. IV, page 42. Bayley's *Gujarat*, page 150, footnote, *Vir Vinod*, Vol. I. Page 328.

of Mewar contiguous to Gujarat was to be attached to Gujarat; and Mewar proper, Ajmer and Ahirwara, to Malwa.

In pursuance of this treaty, a simultaneous attack was made by the allied kings of Malwa and Gujarat the following year (A.D. 1457). Qutb-ud-din advanced towards Kumbhalgarh, while Mahmud Khilji advanced towards Chitor and reached Mandsaur. The Maharna wanted to dispose of Mahmud first; but finding that Qutb-ud-din had come near Kumbhalgarh, advanced to meet him first. Qutb-ud-din had chosen a strong position and the Maharana, after an indecisive action, fell back on a better position flanked by his native hills. Qutb-ud-din encouraged, advanced and an engagement took place which lasted for two days. After the first day's engagement, both armies retired to their camps for the night: the dead bodies were cremated or buried, and the wounded were tended. With the break of day the battle was renewed, and as the Maharana's army had the support of the hills behind them, while the Sultan's army was in the open, the latter suffered severely and was driven out of the field completely vanquished. The Sultan had to fight hard for his life and eventually retired in safety. Thus, though the Maharana suffered heavy losses, the Sultan was defeated and had to return to Gujarat.

Ferishta (Vol. IV, page 42) says that the Sultan on receiving 14 mds. of gold loaded on two elephants and some other things as presents made peace with the Maharana and returned home! This is Ferishta's way of glossing over a defeat. For, Ferishta does not state what 'seasonable donation' the Sultan of Malwa, the ally of the Gujarat King, received as his share of the spoils of war or offering of peace. It is hardly possible to believe that this powerful combination of two monarchs, each burning with a desire completely to crush the common foe, and having solemnly signed a treaty with the express object of dividing the Maharana's territory among themselves should invade the enemy's country from both sides and open the campaign with such confidence and pride, achieve a triumphant victory and yet the net result of it should be the gain to only one of the allies, of 14 mds. of gold, two elephants and some non-descript things!!! It is conceivable that the Sultan took away with him the spoils of some of the temples destroyed by him and the plunder of Sirohi; and some annalist has described the gold and the non-descript things as *nazrana* or tribute. The *Mirati Sikandari* says that three months after this, the Maharana invaded Nagor, when Qutb-ud-din again came to Mewar, and after plundering some villages returned to Ahmedabad. It is difficult to believe that if the Maharana had been defeated in this war, he should have dared to attack Nagor within three months of his defeat; or, that Qutb-ud-din who had been victorious, would have retired satisfied after indulging in a little plundering freak without exacting substantial penalty, or otherwise taking severe revenge for this presumption on the part of the Maharana.

The *Mirati Sikandari*, indeed, says that the Sultan of Mandu returned home, having received from the Rana, the district of Mandsaur and several other parganas adjacent to the territories of Malwa. That the victor should get only a little gold and the spectator, whole districts of the country of the vanquished! Another historian, however, comes nearer the truth. "*Tarikhi Alfi* seems rather to intimate that

Qutb-ud-din made his own terms and left Mahmud to shift for himself."—Bayley's Gujarat, page 151, foot-note. *Rasik Priya*, the commentary on *Gita Govind*, distinctly states that the two kings were defeated and driven out of Mewar by the valiant Maharana. The Chitor *Kirtisthambha* inscription of A.D. 1460, verse 141, states that the Maharana completely defeated the combined armies of Gujarat and Malwa.

The King of Malwa too retired to his territory severely defeated by the Maharana's forces. Though he made several attempts, he was neither able to recover the territory previously conquered and joined to Mewar by Maharana Kumbha, nor to conquer any part of the Maharana's country.[24] He had been so often defeated that after this unsuccessful attempt to retrieve his fallen fortunes, he gave up all hope of success against the Maharana: and though he lived for ten years after this defeat, he never again thought of invading Mewar.[25]

---

24. Ferishta says (Vol IV, page 224) that Mahmud left for Mandalgarh on 26 Muharram, H. 861 (A.D. 1856), and took it on 25 Zilhiji, H. 862 (1458 A.D.)! It is further stated that Mahmud advanced towards Chitor on 5 Muharram H. 863 (A.D. 1458) and sent his son, Prince Ghayas-ud-din, towards Bhilwara, and that the Prince after a severe action took the fort of Kasundi and then returned to Mandu to join his father. Is return home without concluding a triumphant peace, a sign of victory?
25. In S. 1518 (A.D. 1461) Mahmud Khilji did indeed, go towards Kumbhalgarh but dared not attack it. Ferishta says that he passed on to Dungarpur, received two lakhs of rupees from the Raja, as *Faujkharch* and returned to Mandu.—*Ferishta*, Vol. IV, page 225.

WARS WITH THE SULTANS OF MALWA AND GUJARAT 79

Sultan Qutb-ud-din of Gujarat did not long survive[26] this defeat. He died on the 25th of May, A.D. 1459 and was succeeded by Daud Shah in the following year.

In A.D. 1458, reports reached the Maharana that the Mussalmans had begun to kill cows in Nagor. To punish the wrong-doers, he started with fifty thousand horsemen to attack Nagor. After putting thousands of Mussalmans to the sword, he captured the fort and carried away a number of elephants, horses and other valuables as spoils of war. The Khan of Nagor fled to the Court of the Sultan of Ahmedabad.[27]

After a few months, the Sultan of Gujarat invaded Sirohi with a large army. The Maharao of Sirohi retired to the hills of Kumbhalgarh. The Gujarat army after plundering Sirohi, went after the Maharao. The Maharana hearing of this, advanced with his Rajputs and defeated the Sultan, who, fled to his capital.[28]

Smarting under the disgrace of this fresh defeat, Sultan Qutb-ud-din collected a powerful army and started to attack Kumbhalgarh. He came to Sirohi and after plundering that

---

26. Brigg's *Ferishta*, Vol. IV, page 43.
27. *Ferishta* (Vol. IV, p. 43) says that as Qutb-ud-din, Sultan of Gujarat was, at the time engaged in a course of debauchery, the prime minister Imad-ul-mulk collecting an army made one march from Ahmedabad but had to stay there for a month to prepare equipments. Hearing, however, that the Maharana had returned to Chitor the Gujarat army too returned to Ahmedabad.
28. *Ferishta* says that the Sultan finding Kumbhalgarh impregnable, returned to his capital—Vol. IV, p. 43.

country, advanced towards Kumbhlagarh. The Maharana came out of the fort, and attacked and defeated him.[29] The Sultan retreated towards Malwa and thence returned to his Capital.

---

29. *Vir Vinod*, Vol. I, p. 333.

Eleven

Death of Maharana Kumbha

Maharana Kumbha's death took place in A.D. 1468. Sometime before his death, Kumbha's mind showed signs of derangement, and he sometimes talked incoherently. It is said that Maharana Kumbha one day left Kumbhalgarh to visit *Eklingji*. As he arrived near the temple, a cow standing by began to dance, making a long loud sound, usually made when cows are happy. The Maharana said nothing at the time, but on return to Kumbhalmer, in a Durbar the next day, he suddenly raised his hand holding a sword and said कामधेनु तंडव करिय. After a little while, someone made a submission to the Maharana in connection with some business. The Maharana only repeated कामधेनु तंडव करिय. This continued for some days. The nobles and those around the Maharana, seeing this mental derangement of their monarch, became uneasy. The Maharana's younger son Rai Mal mustered up courage and asked the Maharana as to why he repeated those words so often. The Maharana got angry with Rai Mal and ordered that he be banished from Mewar. Rai Mal went away to Idar, as he had been married to the daughter of Bhān, younger brother of Raja Naraindas of that place. No one now dared expostulate with the Maharana.

It is said that an astrologer had told Maharana Kumbha that he would die by the hand of a Charan,[1] whereupon the Maharana expelled the whole of the *Charan* community from Mewar and confiscated their lands. One of them, however, in the guise of a Rajput had remained with a Rajput Sardar; and he now told the Sardar that he understood the reason why the Maharana repeated those words, and that he could make the Maharana stop repeating them. The Sardar took him to the Maharana and introduced him as a relation of his. The Maharana, as was his habit, repeated कामधेनु तंडव करिय, when the Charan got up and confronting the Maharana, recited the following *Chhappaya* (short poem).

जद धर पर जोवती दीठ नागोर धरंती ।
गायत्री संग्रहण देख मन मांही डरंती ॥
सुरकोटी तेतीस आण नीरंता चारो ।
नहिं चरंत पीवंत मनह करती हंकारो ॥
कुंभेण राण हणिया कलम, आजंस उर डर उतरिय ।
तिण दीह द्वार शंकर तणै, कामधेनू तंडव करिय ॥1॥

---

1. A community, the members of which write poetry, are constant companions of the Rajputs, and sing their brave deeds.

"Seeing that cows were killed in Nagor, *gāyatri* (cow) was in great fright. Thirty-three crores of gods used to bring grass and water for her, but she neither ate nor drank anything. When Rana Kumbha after killing Mussalmans (conquering Nagor) has given protection of the cows, then the cow has become delighted and dances with joy at the door of Shankar (Mahadeva)."

The Maharana on hearing the recitation, said to the reciter: "You are no Rajput: you are a *Charan*, but we are very pleased with you." The man confessed that he was a *Charan*, and interceding for his brethren, begged the Maharana to permit their return to Mewar and to restore their lands. The Maharana granted the request.[2] The Maharana, from that day, gave up repeating those words; but his mind had been affected, and he was sometimes incoherent in his talk. While he was in this state of mind, and was one day seated on the edge of a masonry tank near the temple of Mamadeva Kumbhaswami) to the north-east of Katargarh in Kumbhalmer, which he had built ten years before, his eldest son Udai Singh, stole up to him and treacherously stabbed him to death.[3]

The motive for this wicked deed might be the fear that the banished prince Rai Mal might be restored to favour and possibly block the miscreant's way to the throne; or, Kumbhá's enemies, unable to overcome him by force, put up his son to do the wicked deed, promising him assistance to

---

2. *Vir Vinod*, Vol. I, p. 333.
3. *Vir Vinod*, Vol. I, p. 333.

get the throne, as was done in the case of Maharana Ajit Singh of Marwar in the 18th century, when his son, Abhai Singh, was persuaded to get his father murdered. Udái Karan is known in history as 'Udo the *Hatiáro*.'

Maharana Kumbha left eleven[4] sons: Udai Singh, Rai Mal, Nagraj, Gopal Singh, Askarana, Amar Singh, Govin Das, Jait Singh, Mahráwan, Khshetra Singh and Achaldas. One of his daughters, Ramábai, was married to the Yadava Raja Mandlik of Sorath.[5]

The Kumbhalgarh Inscription, verse 251, shows that Maharana Kumbha had married several queens. Two of them, Kumbhaldevi and Apurvadevi, are mentioned in the Chitor *Kirtisthambha* Inscription, as well as in *Rasikpriya*—Kumbha's commentary on *Gita Govind*.

Thus, after a reign of 35 years—a reign full of glory and splendour—Kumbhá departed from this world, leaving behind him, a name which is honoured in history, and remembered to this day as that of one of the greatest sovereigns who ever ruled in India. The Kumbhalgarh Inscription says:—"He was the root of the tree of righteousness, home of virtue and purity, support of wealth, birthplace of truth, abode of prowess, limit of constancy and fortitude, and a representative of *Kalpadruma* (the tree in Heaven which grants all desires). His charities were greater than those of the famous Rajá Bhoj and Karan."

---

4. *Vir Vinod*, Vol. I, p. 335. Mehta Nainsi gives the names of only five.
5. Jāwar Inscription of the Temple of Ramaswami of V.S. 1554 (A.D. 1497).

Maharana Kumbha

Hindupati, Aryakulakamal Divakar. Raj Rajeshwara,
His Highness Maharaja Dhiraj Maharana Sahib, Sir Sir Bhupal Singhji
Bahadur, G.C.S.I. of Mewar

Jug Mandir Palaces–Pichola Lake, Udaipur

Pichola Lake and Udaipur

Rawat Chonda

Rao Jodha, the founder of Jodhpur

Kumbhalgarh

Katargarh and the Vedi

Chitorgarh

Ranpur Temple

Tower of Victory, Chitor (*Kirtisthambha*)

Eklingji Temples

Rao Ran Mal of Mandor

Maharana Pratap

Twelve

Kumbha's Achievements

Maharana Kumbha's military achievements, of which any sovereign might be proud, have not often been surpassed in India. His high moral culture prevented him from emulating the deeds of a Timur or an Alla-ud-din Khilji, and carrying fire and sword from one end of the country to the other. The elevated spiritual plane on which he lived made it repugnant to him to engage in aggressive wars with his neighbours. His genius was equal to achieving far greater feats of military glory than what he accomplished, but his heart, susceptible to the finer feelings of humanity, abhorred all unnecessary bloodshed, ruin and destruction, and he undertook only such military operations as were absolutely necessary for the protection of his country, or, as duty enjoined, to punish evil-doers. Fortune constantly smiled on him: he was ever victorious in war. Inscriptions found in Chitor, Kumbhalgarh, Ránpur and Abu show that he defeated all his enemies, reduced some of them to be his vassals and incorporated portions of the territories of others with his own. He captured Bundi,[1] Bamaodá[2] and conquered the whole of Hārāváti[3] (country of the Hārā Rajputs).

He captured and incorporated with his dominions (Mewar) the towns of Mandalgarh,[4] Shatpur[5] (now called Khatkar), Khatoo,[6] Jana[7] and Chatsoo,[8] and wrested from its Muslim rulers, the whole of the district of Toda[9] and Ajmer.[10]

He annexed the Sapādalaksha[11] country including Sambhar, and imposed a tax on the salt produced there. He also levied a tax on the 'salt mines' at Didvāna,[12] and

---

1. Rānpur Temple Inscription in the Archaeological Survey of India: Annual Report for 1907-08, pp. 214–17.
2. Kumbhalgarh Inscription (unpublished) in the Udaipur Museum, verse 262.
3. Kaviraj Shyamaldas' *Vir Vinod*, p. 335. Also Kumbhalgarh Inscription, Verse 264.
4. Kumbhalgarh Inscription in the Udaipur Museum, V. 263. The inscription calls the place Mandalkar. It was taken from the Hārā Rajputs of Bambaodá.
5. Kumbhalgarh Inscription, V. 264.
6. Rānpur Temple Inscription. The town of Khatoo is now in the Jaipur State. It is famous for its red stone quarries.
7. Rānpur Temple Inscription. Jana is unidentifiable.
8. *Ibid*. Chatsoo is also in the Jaipur State now.
9. *Eklinga Mahatmya*, Sloka 157.
10. Rānpur Temple Inscription. Ajmer was taken by the Maharana from the Sultan of Gujarat.
11. Chitor Tower of Victory Inscription, Verse 5. A part of the inscription is published in Cunningham's Archaeological Survey Report, Vol. XXIII. Also Kumbhalgarh Inscription, V. 261.
12. *Ibid*, V. 6.

conquered the city of Naraina.[13] He conquered Naradiyanagar (Narwar)[14] and reduced to submission the ruler of Shodhyanagari,[15] Yagnapur[16] (Jahazpur in Mewar), Malpura, Yoginipur[17] (Jawar) and Dungarpur, driving out from the last place, Rao Gopal.[18] He burnt down Vrandāvatipur (Bundi)[19] and captured the hill fort of Gargarāt.[20] He "burnt down Mallaranyapur, Sinhapur and Ratanpur and destroyed several kings."[21] "He killed the enemy and took Mandawar (Mandor)"[22] He conquered Amradadri[23] (Amber) and won the battle of Kotra[24] and took the city of Champāvati.[25]

He conquered Sarangpur,[26] taking "numberless Turk women prisoners and humbled the pride of Mahmud (Khilji), its ruler, who had slain his master and become king of the place."

---

13. *Ibid*, V. 6. Naraina is in Jaipur territory and is the headquarters of the *Dadupanthi* sect of the Hindus.
14. Kumbhalgarh Inscription, V. 246.
15. *Ibid*, V. 248.
16. *Ibid*, V. 253.
17. Kumbhalgarh Inscription, Verse 247.
18. *Ibid*, V. 266-67.
19. Kumbhalgarh Inscription, V. 264
20. *Ibid*, V. 259. Also Ranpur Temple Inscription.
21. *Ibid*, V. 260.
22. Kumbhalgarh Inscription, V. 249.
23. *Ibid*, V. 262.
24. Kumbhalgarh Inscription, 262.
25. *Ibid*, V. 258.
26. Kumbhalgarh Inscription, V. 268. It was in this battle that Sultan Mahmud Khilji of Mandu was taken prisoner by the Maharana.

He conquered Hammirpur, captured its king, Randhir Vicrama,[27] and married his daughter. He captured the hilly country of Vardhaman[28] (Badnor) from the Mers; took Amrdachal and conquered the Jankachal[29] hill from the king of Malwa and built a fort on it. He captured and occupied a part of the territory of the Sultan of Delhi.[30] He also conquered the Gokarna Mountain and subjugated the kingdom of Abu,[31] and built Achalgarh[32] on the top of it, and made the Deora Chief (of Sirohi) his vassal.[33] He conquered Gagroon[34] (now in Kotah territory), destroyed Visalpur[35] and raised to the ground the city of Dhanyanagar.[36] He destroyed Khandela[37] and Vyaspur.[38] He conquered the famous fortress of Ranthambhor.[39] He took away the whole of the wealth and kingdom of Muzaffar[40] (King of Gujarat) and humbled his pride (V. 7); conquered Nagor[41] (in Marwar) and plundered

---

27. Kumbhalgarh Inscription, V. 250.
28. Kumbhalgarh Inscription, V. 254.
29. *Ibid*, verses 256-7.
30. Ranpur Temple Inscription.
31. Chitor Tower of Victory Inscription, Verses 8 to 11.
32. *Ibid*, V. 12.
33. *Eklinga Mahatmya*.
34. Rānpur Temple Inscription.
35. Kumbhalgarh Inscription, V. 265.
36. Chitor Tower of Victory Inscription, V. 25.
37. *Ibid*, V. 253.
38. *Eklinga Mahatmya*.
39. Kumbhalgarh Inscription, V. 261.
40. Chitor Tower of Victory Inscription, V. 7.
41. Chitrograh *Kirtisthambha* Inscription. For invasions of Nagor, *see* Chapter X *supra*.

Jāngaladesa[42] (country to the north-west of Ajmer). He repeatedly defeated the kings of Malwa and Gujarat first singly and then combined, when their allied armies invaded Mewar.[43]

The Rānpur Temple Inscription, line 27, says that his "Title as the Hindu Sultan was proclaimed by the Umbrella of Royalty given (him) by the Sultans protecting Gujarat and the territory of Delhi, which were occupied by his great exploits."[44]

The Chitorgarh *Kirtisthambha* Inscription, V. 146, calls Maharana Kumbha, the chief ornament of the kings of the North, East and West.

TITLES OF MAHARANA KUMBHA

The great achievements of Maharana Kumbha in peace as well as in war—in arms as well as in arts—gained him many titles.

1. The Kumbhalgarh Inscription of A.D. 1460 verse 232, mentions the titles of *Maharaja Dhiraj; Rai Rāyan, Rāné Rao; and Maharana.*

---

42. For a full account of Jāngaladesa, see my paper on Jāngaladesa, published in the *Proceedings of the First Oriental Conference, Poona*, A.D. 1921.
43. Chitorgarh *Kirtisthambha* Inscription, a part of which is given in Cunningham's A.S. Reports Vol. XXIII.
    The *Kirtisthambha* Inscription (verse 17) says that he burnt Gujarat, conquered the ruler of Malwa (Mahmud) and destroyed his pride. Further on (verse 171) Kumbha is styled *Agastyamuni* (swallower) of the armies of the Sultans of Gujarat and Malwa.
44. See Ranpur Inscription of A.D. 1439, in Archaeological Survey of India, Annual Report for 1907–8, p. 216.

2. The *Kirtisthambha* Inscription of A.D. 1460, verse 148, mentions his titles of *Rājguru*, *Dānguru*, *Shailguru* and *Paramguru*. *Rajguru* means the Master of Kings or Rajahs. *Dānguru* means the king or the greatest of the givers. *Shailguru* means Master of the mountains. *Paramguru*, according to the inscription, is the highest preceptor of Rajas or kings.
3. The commentary on *Gita Govind* contains Kumbha's titles of *Chāpguru*, *Todarmal* and *Abhinava Bharatāchārya*. Chāpguru means master of the science of war.
4. *Rasikpriya* says that Maharana Kumbha was called Todarmal as he destroyed like a मल्ल (a giant) great Rajas who were Rulers of men (नरपती) Masters of Cavalry (अश्वपती) and Masters of elephants (गजपती). The *Kirtisthambha* Inscription, verse 177, also calls Kumbha, *Todarmal*.

Thirteen

Kumbha's Monuments

Kumbha was a great commander and a great sovereign. He not only greatly extended the boundaries of Mewar but immensely strengthened its defences and adorned it with works of art. Colonel Tod says: "He triumphed over the enemies of his race, fortified his country with strong-holds, embellished it with temples, and with the super-structure of her fame laid the foundations of his own."[1] He re-populated Vasantapur, and built seven lakes near it in the vicinity of Anhalkund of Vashishta[2] in Sirohi (near Abu).

FORTS

Of the 84 fortresses constructed for the defence of Mewar, 32 were built[3] by Kumbha. He fortified the passes between

---

1. *Annals and Antiquities of Rajasthan*, Vol. I, p. 290.
2. Chitorgarh *Kirtisthambha* Inscription, verses 8 and 9.
3. *Vir Vinod*, Vol. I, p. 334. Also Tod's *Rajasthan*, Vol. I, p. 289.

the Western frontier of Mewar and Abu and erected the fort of Vasanti near Sirohi. He built the fort of Machan to defend the Shera Nullá and Devagarh against the Mers of Aravalli. He built the fort of Kolana, near Amba Bhawani, and the fort of Vairat near Badnor, and rebuilt the fort of Ahore (in Mewar), which had been first built by his ancestor Karan Singh, and named it Kailash Meru. He built various other forts to overawe the Bhumiá Bhils of Jarole and Panora, and defined the boundaries of Mewar and Marwar.[4]

ACHALGARH

He constructed in A.D. 1452 (S. 1509, *Magh Sudi* 15th) a citadel on a peak of Mount Abu, since well-known as Achalagarh[5] within the ruined fortress of the ancient Parmar kings of that country, where he often resided.

The traveller would find the ruined towers of Achalgarh buried in the dense masses of clouds that surround him. The first pol (gate) of this ancient fortress is the Hanuman Pol, which is composed of two noble towers built with huge blocks of granite, black with the rude blasts of some 1,000 winters. The towers had been connected at the top by the guard room, and the gate served as the entrance to the lower fort, whose dilapidated walls are discernable up the irregular ascent. Another portal called the Champa Pol, from a noble Champa tree close to it, which was formerly denominated the 'Gate

---

4. Tod's *Rajasthan*, Vol. I, p. 289.
5. *Eklinga Mahatmya*, Sl. 64, and the Chitorgarh Inscription, Plate XXI, Cunningham's A.S.R., Vol. XXIII.

of Wisdom," conducts to the inner fortress. The first object that strikes the view on passing the latter gate is the Jain temple to Paraswanath, erected at the sole expense of a banker of Mándu. Its columns are of the same character as those of the ancient shrine of Ajmer.

The upper ferrous is attributed to Kumbha. But he probably only repaired this, the Donjon of Achalgarh, which with the interior works, is of the most remote antiquity. There are the ruins of a granary, the *Bhandar* of Kumbha Rana, coated within with a very strong cement. Close on the left, is the palace of Oka Rani, his queen, so designated from being of Oka Mandal, (Kathiawar) near the Land's End of the Hindus. A small lake in the keep is called *Sāwan Bhādoon*, and well merits the name of the two chief months of the monsoon; for, in the middle of June it is yet full of water. On the most elevated knoll to the east are the remains of an alarm tower which still bears Kumbha's name. From this point the eye, occasionally piercing the swift-scudding clouds, has glimpses of the ruined altars and palaces of the brave race who on the spot whence I surveyed them, had fought and bled in their defence.[6]

> A blending of all beauties, streams and dells,
> Fruit, foliage, crag, wood, cornfield, mountain, vine,
> And chiefless castles, breathing stern farewells
> From gray, but leafy walls, where Ruin greenly
>   dwells.

---

6. Tod's *Travels in Western India*, p. 94.

An equestrian statue of Maharana Kumbha with those of two other Maharanas and a bigger one of the Purohit or the family priest of Kumbha in a humble straw shed on the descent from Achalgarh to Dilwara still receive divine honours.

Col. Tod describing his visit to Achalgarh, says:—"As the sun dispelled the watery darkness which enveloped us, the landscape of this magic realm was to the last degree imposing, every change of position unfolding some new object. First, Jain shrines of Dilwara (being S. 80° W. six miles distant), backed by the peak of Arbudha Mātā, the Guru Sikra (N. 15° E. four miles), with many other pinnacles scattered over the summit of this fairy land, each with its name and its legend. On the descent, I paid my homage to the representative of one of the worthies of Mewar, an equestrian brass statue of Rana Kumbha, who within these walls had often stood the brunt of war. It was pleasing to witness the homage still rendered within these now desecrated walls, to departed worth; prayers are made, and daily oblations of saffron brought to the defender of Achalgarh, and these not by any of his descendants, who are ignorant of this deed, but by others utterly unconnected with him, actuated by the traditional record of his glory or greatness. The humble straw shed which covers these effigies conveys a finer lesson to the mind than if they were enshrined in marble."[7]

At Abu, Kumbha built the temple of Kumbhaswámi (which still stands) and a large tank named, Ramakund, in

---

7. Tod's *Travels in Western India*, pp. 95-96.

front of it.[8] He excavated four other tanks there.[9] He remitted the pilgrim tax levied at Abu.[10]

KUMBHALGARH

The highest monument of Kumbha's military and constructive genius, however, is the wonderful fortress of Kumbhalgarh or Kumbhalmer, second to none in strategical importance or historical renown. It was to this impregnable fortress that the Maharanas of Mewar always turned their eyes, when, Udaipur became unsafe and Chitor untenable. It is to Kumbhalmer that the Maharanas, from Udai Singh to Raj Singh, sent the royal households, when the entire might of the Moghal Empire was used for the destruction of their country. It was the ambition of Akbar, the greatest of the Moghul Emperors of India to take it, when his hosts, led by the greatest of his generals, the renowned Man Singh of Amber and supported by the armies of the Rathods of Marwar and Bikaner, the Kuchhwahas of Amber (Jaipur) and other Rajput Chiefs, invaded the country of the immortal Pratap.

The cunning of Akbar succeeded in raising against this devoted land most of its Rajput neighbours, and the fortress fell. It was, however, soon recovered by Pratap; and the successors of Akbar—Jahangir with all his vain-glory, and

---

8. Kumbha's Chitorgarh *Kirtisthambha* Inscription (Vs. 12 and 13). Near the Ramakund, stands a statue of the Parmar king Dhárávarsha armed with a bow, and three stone buffaloes.
9. Same.
10. Same.

Aurangzeb with all his craft and cunning—failed to make any impression on this historic fortress. When Prince Khurram, ennobled with the title of Shah Jahan (King of the World), with all the resources that the empire could command, supported by Emperor Jahangir at the base of operations, Ajmer, overran the country of Pratap's noble son, Amra; or when that destroyer of the Moghal Empire, Aurangzeb, collecting the Imperical armies from all parts of the Empire, vainly launched his legions against the chivalrous Maharana Raj Singh in an attempt to deprive this sacred soil of its ancient independence, this strong-hold, the ever memorable Kumbhalgarh, provided shelter to those who were dear to the noble defenders of their fatherland. This fortress, which has played a part in history, seldom rivalled and never surpassed, was the bulwark of Mewar throughout the Moghal rule in India.

> "When they were young and proud,
> Banners on high and battles passed below;
> But they who fought are in a bloody shroud,
> And those which waved are shredless dust ere now,
> And the bleak battlements shall bear no future blow."

Kumbhalgarh and the *Kirtisthambha* (Tower of Victory) at Chitor, are the two pillars on which the fame of Kumbha as a great commander and a great sovereign rests. Kumbhlagarh, situated on the 25°9' N. and 73°35' E, about 60 miles north of Udaipur, stands on a high peak of the most westerly range of the Aravalli hills, on the site of an ancient strong-hold, which, according to tradition, was built by the famous Jain king Samprati, who flourished in the third century[11] of the Christian era. Kumbha began the construction of the fort in S. 1500 (A.D. 1443), and it was completed on the 13th of the dark half of *Chaitra*, S. 1515 (A.D. 1458).[12] It was designed and built by Kumbha's architect Mandana.

Kumbhalgarh is defended by a series of walls with battlements and bastions built on the slopes of a hill, and contains a domed palace and buildings which are reached through several gateways along a winding approach. The palace in it built by Kumbha and rebuilt by the late Maharana Fateh Singh stands 3,568 feet above sea level, and commands a fine panoramic view of the wild and rugged scenery of the Aravallis[13] and the sandy plains of Marwar. Below this peak, on every side, and enclosed within a high battlemented wall, so thick as to allow 8 horsemen to ride abreast, the uneven ground is studded with numerous old temples and reservoirs, barracks for the garrison, grain stores and other domed buildings.

The formidable bastions in the battlemented wall of Kumbhalgarh, as the illustration on the opposite page will show, are peculiar in shape and are so built that the enemy may not be able to scale them by means of ladders. Outside

---

11. Samprati was the second son of Emperor Asoka who died in 236 or 237 B.C. His eldest son Kunal reigned for 8 years and was succeeded by Samprati who also reigned for 8 years.
12. Chitorgarh Inscription, Cunningham's Archæological Survey Report, Vol. XXIII, plate 21.
13. The names of several neighbouring hills are given in the Chitorgarh Inscription as Nila, Shweta, Hemkut, Himvat, Nishad, Gandhamadan.

the fortress, at some little distance on a mound, is a fine temple consisting of a square sanctuary with a vaulted dome and a colonnade of elegant pillars all round. Describing this ancient temple, Col. Tod says:—"The design of this temple is truly classic. It consists only of the sanctuary, which has a vaulted dome and colonnaded portico all round. The architecture is undoubtedly Jain, which is as distinct in character from the Brahminical, as their religion. There is a chasteness and simplicity in this specimen of monotheistic worship, affording a wide contrast to the elaborately sculptured shrines of the Saivas, and other polytheists of India. The extreme want of decoration best attests its antiquity, entitling us to attribute it to that period when Samprati Raja, of the family of Chandragupta, was paramount sovereign over all these regions, (two hundred years before Christ); to whom tradition ascribes the most ancient monuments of this faith, yet existing in Rajasthan and Saurashtra. The proportions and forms of the columns are especially distinct from the other temples, being slight and tapering, instead of massive, the general characteristic of Hindu architecture; while the projecting cornices, which would absolutely deform shafts less slight, are peculiarly indicative of the Takshac architect. A massive monolithic emblem of black marble of the Hindu Jivapitri, had been improperly introduced into the shrine of the worshippers of the 'spirit alone'. Being erected on the rock, and chiselled from the syenite on which it stands, it may bid defiance to time. There was another sacred structure in its vicinity, likewise Jain, but of a distinct character; indeed, offering a perfect contrast to that described. It was three storeys in height; each tier was decorated with numerous massive low columns, resting on a sculptured panelled parapet, and sustaining the roof of each storey, which being very low, admitted but a broken light to break the pervading gloom"[14]

In the central open space of the fort, on a conical hillock, stands the inner fort of Katárgarh. It is crowned with a palace called the *Jháli-ká-Máliá* or the palace of the Jháli queen.

There are seven gates leading up to the fort. The principal (exterior) one, called the Hanumán Pol, from the image of the god Hanuman which with the gates was brought by Kumbhá from Mandor[15] and set up there, faces the south at the head of a road which winds gradually up through the gorge from the town of Kailwara at its base—a place of great historical interest. Between Kailwara and the Hanuman Pol there are two gates, the first being Aret Pol, or barrier thrown across the first narrow ascent about a mile from Kallwara. The second is called the Hulla Pol; the third is the Hanumán Pol, between which and the summit there are four more gates, *viz.*, the Gate of Victory, the Sanguinary Gate, the Gate of Ráma and the Chaugán Pol. Colonel James Tod says: "It would be vain to attempt describing the intricacies of approach to this far-famed abode, whose exterior is delineated by the pencil. A massive wall, with numerous towers and pierced battlements, having a strong resemblance to the Etruscan, enclose a space of some miles extent below, while the pinnacle or *Sikra* rises like the crown of the Hindu Cybele, tier above

---

14. *Annals and Antiquities of Rajasthan*, Vol. I, pp. 670–71.
15. Kumbhalgarh Inscription, v. 3.

tier of battlements, to the summit,[16] which is crowned with the *Badal Mahal* or 'Cloud Palace' of the Rana. Thence, the eye ranges over the sandy deserts and the chaotic mass of mountains which are on all sides, covered with the cactus, which luxuriates amidst the rocks of the Aravalli."

As one ascends the fort hill, there is on the left, *Tārā burj* called after Tara, the heroic consort of prince Prithviraj, son of Rana Rai Mal and grandson of Maharana Kumbha. Before we reach the Chaugan Pol we come to Nārchhāli, a small empty reservoir, from where, it is said, the tiger (nār) and the goat (chhāli) used to drink water together before the fort was built. After crossing the Chaugan Pol, the visitor has to his right the *Topkhānā*, where a cannon is pointed out as a trophy brought from Nagor. Further onwards is *Nava-choki*, which is really a temple dedicated to Navadurga. Here, is a small fragmentary inscription stone in the pavement of the hall floor. Therein, only two names can be traced, *viz.*, those of Mokal, father of Kumbha, and Prayāga, *i.e.* Allahabad. The last gate, as stated above, is the Pāgdā Pol, so called because the Mahārānā here dismounts from his horse before entering the palace.

Just inside the Hanumán Pol on the ridge below the palace is situated the *Vedi*, or the place where the *Yajna* in consecration of the fort was performed by Kumbhá when it was completed. It is a beautiful three-storeyed building of great architectural merit; each tier is decorated with numerous massive low columns, resting on a sculptured

---

16. Tod's *Annals and Antiquities of Rajasthan* (original edition), Vol. I., page 670.

panelled parapet and sustaining the roof of each storey, which being very low, admits but a broken light to break the pervading gloom.

A memorable structure built by Maharana Kumbha, in A.D. 1458, in the gorge below the fort on the brow of the mountain overlooking the pass, is the Mámádeva Temple. The court of the temple is formed by a strong wall enclosing a large area. The interior of this wall was covered with immense slabs of black marble, on which was inscribed the history of Mewar from the time of Guhil, the founder of the royal family, to Maharana Kumbha.

Col. Tod thus describes the state of these tablets when he visited this place on 19 October, A.D. 1819. "What a sight for the antiquary! Not one of the many tablets was entire; the fragments were strewn about, or placed in position to receive the flesh-pots of the sons of Ishmael, the mercenary Rohilla Afghan."[17]

"The tablets and most of the images of the divinities referred to by Tod, which were for long lying utterly uncared for, were removed by Pandit Gaurishankar Ojhá to the Museum at Udaipur. The fragments of the tablets, so far as a through search could bring to light, were picked up and pieced together by him, and can now be easily deciphered there. The importance of these inscriptions can never be overrated. They set forth the history of Mewar from the time of Guhila, the founder of the Udaipur family, to Rana Kumbha."[18]

---

17. *Annals and Antiquities of Rajasthan*, Vol. I, p. 672.
18. Progress Report of the Archæological Survey of India, Western Circle, for 1968–9, by Dr. D.R. Bhandarkar.

Behind the temple of Mamadeva is an *odi*, or raised dais where Tārā, wife of Prince Prithviraj, elder brother of Maharana Sāngā, used to shoot tigers.

On quitting the temple of Mamadeva, attention is attracted by a simple monumental shrine on the opposite side of the valley, and almost in the gorge of the pass. "It was most happily situated, being quite isolated, overlooking the road leading to Marwar, and consisted of a simple dome of very moderate dimensions, supported by columns, without any intervening object to obstruct the view of the little monumental alter arising out of the centre of the platform. It was the Sybilline temple of Tivoli in miniature. To it, over rock and ruin, I descended. Here, repose the ashes of the Troubadour of Mewar, the gallant Prithviraj, and his heroine wife, Tara Bai,[19] whose lives and exploits fill many a page of the legendary romances of Mewar."[20]

In the shrine is a memorial stone on which various small figures are sculptured on each one of its four sides, with small inscriptions above, descriptive of them. Thus, *e.g.*, on the east side it bears five figures, the central one of which rides of horse. He is called Prithirajaji, *i.e.* Prithviraj, and the horse Sāhanadivā. Immediately on his right is Tárádê (Tārā Devi) and further Bai Pāmāde. On his left also there are two figures, the names of which are, however, gone. Memorial stones

---

19. This fair 'star' (Tārā) was the daughter of Rao Soortan, the chieftain of Badnor. For some account of Tarabai and Prince Prithviraj see my monograph on 'Maharana Sanga', Chapter IV. Prithviraj was one of the most heroic Rajputs that adorn the history of Rajputana.
20. Tod's *Rajasthan*, Vol. I, p. 673.

mark the places where ladies became *Sati* on the funeral pyres of their husbands, and this particular stone commemorates the fact that Tārādé (Tārā Devi) and Pāmāde became Sati on the death of prince Prithviraj.

Near the Māmādeva Temple, Maharana Kumbha built a large *Kunda* (reservoir of water), at the edge of which Kumbha was saying his prayers when he was treacherously stabbed by his son, Udá the *Hatiáro* (parricide). Kumbhá built the Kumbhaswami Temple in the fort and constructed a lake by it, and laid out a garden.[21]

CHITORGARH

Kumbha strengthened the defences[22] of Chitor and built seven[23] of its gates—the Rampol with circular bastions, after Ráma the great hero of the Solar dynasty, the *Surya Vamsa*, of which the Maharana of Mewar is the head. This *Pol* was partly dismantled by Emperor Shah Jahan. The remains of its plinth are handsomely carved with figure friezes; the Hanumánpol, called after the temple of this god; the Bairavapol, since associated with the name of Bhairavadas Solanki, who fought bravely and was killed at that spot in the

---

21. *Kumbhalgarh* Inscription, verses 130, 131 and 143.
22. The Chitorgarh *Kirtisthambha* Inscription, verse 26, Verse 183 says that in Kartik S. 1507 (A.D. 1450) Kumbha built a new bastion with battlements. The architect employed by Maharana Kumbha in Chitor was Natha, brother of Mandana, who had built Kumbhalgarh, *vide*, p. 38.—S. R. Bhandarkar's Report of a Tour in Rajputana, etc. 1907.
23. *Kirtisthambha Inscription*, verses 36–42 and 125.

battle against Sultan Bahadur Shah of Gujarat in A.D. 1534–35; Lakshmipol, Chāmundápol, Tarapol and Rajpol.[24]

Maharana Kumbha built the present road[25] up the hill by which carriages can go up to the fort. Before his time there was only a foot-path.

Maharana Kumbha also built a Rama Kund at Chitor[26] and several stepped wells and reservoirs for storing water.

TOWER OF VICTORY

Kumbha's *Jaya Sthambha* (Tower of Victory), also called the *Kirtisthambha* (Tower of Fame) in Chitorgarh is another monument of his genius and a great ornament to that far-famed fortress.

This celebrated Tower of Victory was erected to commemorate the victory which Maharana Kumbha had obtained over Sultan Mahmud Khilji I of Mandu in A.D. 1438, when Mandu was conquered, and its Sultan brought captive, and kept a prisoner in Chitor for six months.

An inscription[27] in the perforated window in the second window in the second storey of the Tower of Victory offering the obeisance of the architect Jaitra and his two sons, Nāpā and Punjā, to god Samaddhishwar dated *Phalgun* Sud 5th, V.S. 1499 (A.D. 1442) shows that the second storey was completed in that year. The Tower was completed in A.D. 1449; for the

---

24. The last four pols are now called Lakshmanpol, Jorlapol, Ganeshpol and Pādalpol.
25. The Chitorgarh *Kirtisthambha* Inscription, verses 34–35.
26. Chitor *Kirtisthambha* Inscription, verse 33.
27. Report for A.D. 1921 of the Rajputana Museum, Ajmer, p. 4.

consecration ceremony of the Tower of Victory, as recorded in the 186th verse of the *Prasasti* of the *Jaya Sthambha* took place on *Magh Sud*, 10th, *Pushiya Nakshatra* V.S. 1505 (A.D. 1449).[28] As it took six years to complete the building from the third to the topmost storey it may fairly be inferred that the foundations of the *Jaya Sthambha* must have been laid 2 years before the completion of the second storey, *i.e.* in A.D. 1440.

Describing it, Fergusson says: "A pillar of victory like that of Trojan at Rome, but in infinitely better taste as an architectural object than the Roman example."[29]

Colonel James Tod[30] thus describes it: "The only thing in India to compare with this is the Kootab Minar at Delhi, but though much higher, it is of a very inferior character. This column is one hundred and twenty feet in height; the breadth of each face at the base is thirty-five feet, and at the summit, immediately under the cupola, seventeen feet and a half. It stands on an ample terrace, forty-two feet square. It has nine distinct storeys, with openings at every face of each storey, and all these doors have colonnaded porticos." Each storey is lighted by trellis windows, and the angles and recesses not intersected by steps are utilised for statues and ornaments. The exterior surface is broken up into nine principal divisions each furnished with its windows, balustrades, eaves or Chhajjas and emphasised by columns, plasters and numberless horizontal hands and cornices. A stair passes up the tower though its nine storeys but the peculiarity consists in its

---

28. *Kirtisthambha* (Tower of Victory) Inscription, V. 185.
29. *History of Indian and Eastern Architecture*, page 253.
30. *Annals and Antiquities of Rajasthan*, Vol. II., page 761.

winding alternately through a central well and a gallery formed round it. The two upper storeys are open and more ornamental than those below. The whole of the lower is covered with architectural ornaments and sculptures to such an extent as to leave no plain parts, while at the same time, this mass of decoration is kept so subdued that it in no way interferes either with the outline or the general effect of the pillar. It is built chiefly of compact lime-stone and the quartz rock on which it stands, which takes the highest polish: indeed, there are portions possessing the hardness, and exhibiting the fracture, of Jasper. It is one mass of sculpture; of which a better idea cannot be conveyed than in the remark of those who dwell about it, that it contains every object known to their mythology.

The nineth *khand* or 'storey' which, as I have stated, is seventeen feet and a half square, has numerous columns supporting a vault in which is sculptured Kanaya (Krishna) in the *Rasmandala* (celestial sphere), surrounded by the *gopis*, or muses, each, holding a musical instrument, and in a dancing attitude. Beneath this is a richly-carved scroll fringed with the *sarus*, the *phenicopteros* of ornithology. Around this chamber had been arranged, on black marble tablets,[31] the

---

31. A copy of this and the Kumbhalgarh Inscription of Rana Kumbha was taken by a pandit on *Phagun Vadi* 7th, S. 1735 (A.D. 1679), when five tablets of this, and one of the Kumbhalgarh Inscriptions were in existence. Unfortunately, ony two tablets of this former inscription are now to be found, but two more tablets and a fragment of the third of the Kumbhalgarh Inscription have been recovered. The Kumbhalgarh Inscription originally consisted of five tablets and the Chitorgarh of seven or more. The Chitorgarh

whole genealogy of the Rānās of Chitor; but the Goths have broken or defaced all save one slab.

"I gazed," says Colonel Tod,[32] "until the sun's last beam fell upon this ringlet of Chitor illuminating its glory and grief-worn aspect, like a lambent gleam lighting up the face of sorrow. Who could look, on this lovely, this majestic column, which tells in language more easy of interpretation than the tablets within, of

'.........deeds which should not pass away,
And names which must not wither,'

and withold a sigh for its departed glories?"

Colonel Tod further says: "The view from this elevated spot was superb, extending far into the plains of Malwa. The lightning struck and injured the dome[33] some years ago, but generally there is no semblance of decay, though some shoots of *peepul* have rooted themselves where the bolt of Indra fell.

It is said to have cost ninety lakhs of rupees, or near a million sterling, and this is only one of the many magnificent

---

Inscription states that it was completed on Monday the *Margshir Vadi* 5th, S. 1517 and Saka year 1382 (A.D. 1460). The author of the inscription was a Brahman named Atri, who was well-versed in Logic, Vedanta, Veda, Mimansa and Sahitya. He was the son of Keshava, called Jhoting, and grandson of Narahari and great grandson of Somanath of the Bhragu family. Atri having died, the inscription was completed by his son Mahesh, a poet. The Maharana gave him as reward, two elephants, two *chanwars* with gold handles, and a white umbrella (छत्र).

32. *Annals and Antiquities of Rajasthan*, Vol. II, p. 756.
33. The old injured dome was removed and the present bulbons dome constructed by Maharana Swarup Singh after A.D. 1839.

works of Maharana Kumbha within Chitor, the temples to Krishna, the lake called Cooram Sagar, the temple[34] and fountain to Kookgreoo (Kukreshwar), Mahadeva having been erected by him."

TEMPLES

Maharana Kumbha built many grand temples in Mewar. In each of the two celebrated forts of Mewar,—Chitor and Kumbhalgarh—as also in Abu, Maharana Kumbha built a Kumbhaswami temple.

Kumbhaswami Temple

Of the three, the magnificent Kumbhaswami temple at Chitor 'which was like the crown of the world,[35]' appears to have been built in V.S. 1505 (A.D. 1448); for we find inscriptions dated the V.S. 1505 (A.D. 1448) of Maharana Kumbha on the pedestals of some of the images in the niches of the *Sabhāmandap* (domed hall) in front of the temple proper. This temple of Kumbhaswami dedicated to Lord Krishna, is said to have been constructed with the materials brought from the ruins of the ancient shrines at Nagari,[36] situated 7 miles

---

34. This temple was originally built by Raja Kukreshwar, who excavated the fountain in A.D. 755 (*Magh* Sud 5th, S. 811 (Thursday).—Archæological Survey Report, Vol. XXIII, p. 113.
35. Kumbha's Commentary on *Gita Govind*, Sloka 63.
36. For a full account of this city of remote antiquity, see Archæological Survey of India, Vol. Vi, for 1872–73 A.D. pp. 196–226 and Col. Erskine's *Gazetteer of Udaipur*. Some very ancient coins were found at Nagara or Nagari, which are unique in type and many date several centuries B.C.

from Chitor. It consists of a large square porch supporting a low pyramidal roof on massive pillars in front of a *sanctuary* with a stately *Sikra*, majestic both in outline and size. Over the front entrance is a sculptured stone figure of a man wearing ornaments which may be intended for Maharana Kumbha himself.

To the west of the temple are two reservoirs, 125 feet long, 50 feet wide, and 50 feet deep, of large blocks of stone built it is said early in the fifteenth century A.D. to commemorate the marriage of the daughter of Rana Mokul called the 'Lal Bai' (or Ruby of Mewar) with Achil Singh Kheechi of Gagroon. These reservoirs, which were filled with *ghi* and oil for distribution to the guests at the wedding, are still known by the names of '*Ghi Baori*' and '*Tel Baori*.'

This temple has carvings in parts of its exterior walls and roofs which are generally found in 'Buddhist buildings.'

This temple stands to the south of *Badal Mahal* and is described as the temple of Govind Shyama by Abul Fazal in his *Akbarnama*. It was built by Maharama Kumbha in Sambat 1505 (A.D. 1448). By its side, Maharana Kumbha built the temple of *Adi Varāh*[37] which is now wrongly called Miranbai's temple.

Rānpur Temple

Though the temple of Kumbha Shyām at Chitorgarh is a noteworthy one, yet of all the temples erected or resuscitated

---

37. Chitor *Kirtisthambha* Inscription, V. 31.

in Kumbha's time, the Chaumukha Temple of Rānpur is the most important. It was erected in the Sadri Pass leading from the western descent of the highlands of Mewar, and is dedicated of the highlands of Mewar, and is dedicated to Rishabnath or Rishabdeva, the first of the Jaina *Tirthankaras*. It is situated in a spot evidently selected for its natural beauties.

Rānpur lies in the Desuri district of the Marwar State. Originally it was a part of Mewar, when Godwar was incorporated with it. When, however, Godwar was ceded in the 18th century to Marwar; Desuri, and with it Rānpur, ceased to be a part of the Maharana's dominions. Rānpur is a village lying 6 miles to the south of Sādari, the chief town of Desuri. It is situated in a valley piercing the western flank of Adābāla hills which name has been corrupted into Aravalli.[38] A more lovely spot is not to be found in the whole of Marwar.

Rānpur contains several temples, the most celebrated of which is the Chaumukha Temple dedicated to the first Jaina *Tirthankara* Adinath or Rishabdeva, and because of it, Rānpur is one of the five sacred places in Marwar. Streams of Jain pilgrims visit it all the year round. It was built by Maharana Kumbha's favourite, Dhāranaka, in V.S. 1496 (A.D. 1439), and was designed by the architect Dipaka. It is four storeys high including the underground vault and is supported by numerous columns of granite upwards of forty-feet high. The interior is inlaid with mosaics of cornelian and agate.

The temple is called Chaumukha because the principal figure is a group of four images placed on a pedestal back

---

38. Dr. D.R. Bhandarkar's article in the Annual Report of the Archaeological Survey of India, 1907–8, p. 205.

to back so as to face the four cardinal directions. The images are of white marble, and all of Rishabdeva. "The upper storey also contains a similar shrine accessible by four doors opening from the terraced roofs of the building. The lower and principal shrine has no door, as is very often the case with Jain temples, but only a small porch called *Mukhamanadapa*. Further, on a lower level, is a Sabhā-Mandapa or open assembly hall, on each side approached by a *nāl* or flight of stairs. Outside this flight of stairs is an open porch, and above, a closed one popularly known as *Nāl-Mandapa*. Each one of the open porches is accessible by another flight of stairs; but of the latter, that facing the west, contains far more stairs than the others and consequently the entrance on the west is considered to be the principal one. Facing the sides of each of the *Mukhamandapas* of the principal or Chaumukha shrine is a *mādar* or larger subsidiary shrine; and facing each *Sabhamandapa* is a smaller subsidiary shrine or *Khūnt-ra Mandar*, so called because they stand exactly on the *nāsaks* or angles formed by lines drawn through the centres of the *Sabhamandapas*. The sides of the temple, between the *mādars* and the entrances are occupied by *bhāmtis* or ranges of cells for images, each with a pyramidal roof of its own but without any partitioning walls. They contain inscriptions belonging to the first half of the 16th Century and recording the erection of *devakulikās* or cells by Jain devotees, most of whom were Oswals, hailing from Pātan, Cambay and other places."[39]

---

39. Dr. D.R. Bhandarkar's articles in the Annual Report of the Archaeological Survey of India for 1907–8, p. 211.

112   MAHARANA KUMBHA

Fergusson says that Maharana Kumbha, "during his long and prosperous reign filled his country with beautiful buildings, both civil and ecclesiastical. Amongst others he built this temple of Rānpur,[40] situated in a lonely and deserted glen, running into the western slope of the hills below his favourite fort of Kumbhalgarh. Notwithstanding long neglect, it is still nearly perfect, and is the most complicated and extensive Jaina temple, I have myself ever had an opportunity of inspecting."[41]

"From the plan it would be perceived that it is nearly a square, 200 ft. by 225 ft., exclusive of the projections on each face. In the centre stands the great shrine, not, however, occupied, as usual, by one cell, but by four; or rather four great niches, in each of which is placed a statue of Adinatha, or Rishabdeva, the first and greatest of the Jaina *Tirthankars*. Above this are four other niches, similarly occupied, opening on the terraced roofs of the building. Near the four angles of the court are four smaller shrines, and around them, or on each side of them, are 20 domes supported by about 420 columns; 4 of these domes—the central ones of each group—are 3 storeys in height, and tower over the others; and one—that facing the principal entrance—is supported by the very unusual number of 16 columns, and is 36 ft. in diameter, the others being only 24 ft. Light is admitted to the building by four uncovered courts, and the whole is surrounded by a

---

40. "It is one of the largest edifices existing, and cost upwards of a million sterling, towards which Kumbha contributed eighty thousand pounds"—Tod's *Rajasthan*, Vol. I., p. 289.
41. *History of Indian and Eastern Architecture*.

range of cells, many of them now unoccupied, each of which has a pyramidal roof of its own. "The internal effect of this forest of columns may be gathered from the view taken across one of its courts; but it is impossible that any view can reproduce the endless variety of perspective and the play of light and shade which results from the disposition of the pillars and of the domes, and from the mode in which the light is introduced. A wonderful effect also results from the number of cells, most of them containing images of *Tirthankars*, which everywhere meet the view. Besides the twelve in the central *Sikhars*, there are eighty-six cells of very varied form and size surrounding the interior, and all their facades more or less adorned with sculpture.......... The beauty of detail—no two pillars in the whole building being exactly alike—the grace with which they are arranged, the tasteful mixture of domes of different heights with flat ceilings and the mode in which the light is introduced combine to produce an excellent effect. Indeed, I know of no other building in India of the same class that leaves so pleasing an impression or affords so many hints for the graceful arrangement of columns in an interior.

"Besides its merits of design, its dimensions are by no means to be despised; it covers altogether about 48,000 square ft., or nearly as much as one of our ordinary mediæval cathedrals; and, taking the basement into account, is nearly of equal bulk; while in amount of labour and of sculptural decorations it far surpasses any."[42]

---

42. *History of Indian and Eastern Architecture*, pp. 241–2.

An inscription in the temple incised on a slab of white marble measuring 1'1" broad by 3 feet 3 inches high, and containing 47 lines of Sanskrit prose built up in a pillar close to the entrance of the main shrine on its right, gives a record of the Guhilot dynasty, and said that the temple is dedicated to Yugadisvara, another name of Rishabdeva or Adinath, also called here Chaturmukha and says that it was built in the time and by order of Maharana Sri Kumbhakaran by Dhārnaka who is described as *paramarhata*, a devout Jain and ornament of the *Prāgvata Vamsa*, which is now known as Porvāda Mahajan community. His mother's name is given as Kamala De, and father's as Kurāpal. The inscription says that a Jaina banker Gunaraj helped in the erection of the temple, and that the town of Rānpur was founded and called after his name by Maharana Kumbhakaran.

The temple was known at the time as *Chaturmukha-Yugadiscara Vihāra*, i.e. a temple of four-faced Rishabnatha. Line 46 of the inscription gives the name of the architect as Dipāka, and mentions that Dharanaka built temples at Ajāhari, Sālera and Pindarvataka, modern Pindavārā. Local tradition has it that the temple was built by two brothers Dhanna (corruption of Dharnaka)[43] and Ratna of the Porvad caste and residents of Nāndiya in the Sirohi State. They left Nandiya and settled at Mālgad which was situated to the south of Rānpur, high upon a hill. They erected a temple at

---

43. A descendant of Ratna, 14 generations removed from him, named Nath Mal Sah was living in A.D. 1907 in Ghanerav, to which town, Dhanna and Ratna had moved.

Mādadá, which came to be known as Rānpur, because the land occupied by the temple was purchased by them from Maharana Kumbha, who stipulated that the place should bear his name, Rān being an abbreviation of Rānā.

The temple was designed by one Dipaka or Dipa, a Sompura Brahmin of Mundātā in the following circumstances. One night at Maglad, Dhanna saw a celestial car in his dream. He called several Sompuras (architects) and gave them a description of it, and asked them to produce plans thereof. All were rejected except that of Dipa as it was exactly of the type of the celestial car, Dhanna had seen in his dream. It was originally intended to have seven storeys of which only four were completed including the subterranean vault. This non-completion of the building is given as the reason why no descendant of Ratna now shaves his head with a razor.

Eklingji

Eklingji is the Cathedral town of Mewar. And the Maharana, like the ancient Buddhist king of Gāndhāra is the Defender of the Faith and the Head of the Church. Eklingji and Nāthdwara are the two most important religious places in Mewar. The temple of Eklingji is unique in character. Eklingji is the *Ishtdeva* or the god which the Maharanas worship. He is held to be the master or ruler of Mewar and the Maharana his *divan* or chief minister. It is due to this fact, that the Maharana of Udaipur is styled *divan* or *Divanji* in Rajputana. In the war-like songs sung in Rajputana and the poems recited by the bards, *divan* is used in preference to Maharana. The famous poem of Dursaji on the immortal Maharana Pratap, says:[44] — दीठो कोई दीवाण करतो लुटका कटहड़ै! "Has any one seen the Maharana bow his head before the ballustrade in the Mughal Court?"

Early in the 8th century, the sage Hárita conferred on Bappá Ráwal the title of Regent of Eklingji, and to this day the Maharanas of Mewar, as *divans* or regents of Siva, supersede the high priest in his duties and themselves perform the ceremonies when they visit the temple.

Eklingji is situated in a defile about 13 miles north of Udaipur. The road, which has recently been improved, passes over undulating hills, particularly along a valley and over a gorge about two-thirds of the way, beyond which it is more level and surrounded by a number of small lakes which beautify the country. "The hills towering around it on all sides are of the primitive formation, and their scarped summits are clustered with honey-combs. There are abundant small springs of water, which keep verdant numerous shrubs, the flowers of which are acceptable to the deity; especially the *Kiner* or oleander, which grows in great luxuriance on the Aravalli. Groves of bamboo and mango were formerly common, according to tradition; but although it is deemed sacrilege to thin the groves of Bal, the bamboo has been nearly destroyed: there are, however, still many trees sacred to the deity scattered around."[45]

The temple of Eklingji is dedicated to Mahadeva or Siva. Bappa Rawal is said to have built the original temple. It was

---

44. *Maharana Yash Prakāsh*, p. 99.
45. Tod's *Rajasthan*, Vol. I, p. 515.

rebuilt by Maharana Mokal who built a wall round it. Maharana Raimal greatly improved it and installed a four faced image of Siva in it in V.S. 1545 (A.D. 1488).

Maharana Kumbha renovated[46] the temple, constructed the magnificent *Kumbhamandapa* (domed hall) in front of the *sanctum sanctorum* and the *toran* (archway) leading to the mandapa (dome). He presented the temple with the gold flagstaff and numerous Kalus and bestowed on the temple for its maintenance, the four villages of Nagada[47] Kathdāwan, Malak-Khera and Bhimān.[48]

The temple of Eklingji is of an unusual design having a double storied porch and a double storied sanctuary, the former covered by a flat pyramidal roof composed of many hundred circular knobs, the latter roofed by a lofty tower of more than ordinary elaboration.

"It would be difficult to convey a just idea of a temple so complicated in its details. It is of the form commonly styled pagoda, and, like all the ancient temples of Siva, its *sikhara*, or pinnacle, is pyramidal. The various orders of Hindu sacred architecture are distinguished by the form of the *sikhara*, which is the portion springing from and surrounding the perpendicular walls of the body of the temple. The *sikhara* of those of Siva is invariably pyramidal, and its sides vary with

---

46. Kumbhalgarh Inscription verse, 241.
47. Nāgada, in olden days a famous town, was the capital of the rulers of Mewar. It is situated not very far from Eklingji.
48. Tod's *Annals and Antiquities of Rajasthan*, Vol. I, p. 515. The shrine of Eklingji is endowed with twenty-four large villages from the fisc, besides parcels of land from the chieftains.

the base, whether square or oblong. The apex is crowned with an ornamental figure, as a sphynx, an urn, a ball, or a lion, which is called *Kullus*. When the *sikhara* is but the frustum of a pyramid, it is often surmounted by a row of lions, as at Bijolli.

The fane of Eklingji is of white marble and of ample dimensions. Under an open-vaulted temple supported by columns, and fronting the four-faced divinity, is the brazen bull, *nandi*, of the natural size; it is cast, and of excellent proportions. The figure is perfect, except where the shot or hammer of an infidel invader has penetrated its hollow flank in search of treasure. Within the quadrangle are miniature shrines, containing some of the minor divinities. The high priest of Eklingji, like all his order, is doomed to celibacy, and the office is continued by adopted disciples. Of such spiritual descents they calculate sixty-four since the sage Harita, whose benediction obtained for the Guhilot Rajput the sovereignty of Chitor.

The town of Eklingji is separated from Nagada by a lake, which is one of the many artificial waters that beautify the Udaipur valley, and its *bund* or dam was built by Bhogaditya, five generations before Bappa, and has since been frequently repaired. It is shut in by wooded hills, and on its western margin are two interesting temples, both ranking high as specimens of ancient Hindu architecture.

OTHER TEMPLES

Following the example set by Maharana Kumbha, the people of Mewar following different faiths constructed several fine temples and dedicated them to the gods of their worship. In

Rānpur itself, *Porwad mahajan* Vanshisagar's son Kurāpal's son Ratna, and Ratna's sons and grandsons built with Maharana Kumbha's permission in S. 1496 (A.D. 1439), a magnificent *Chaumukha* (four-faced) temple called *Trilokyadipak* (the light of three worlds) dedicated to Yugadishwara. This is one of the notable temples of the Jain faith in India.

Shah Gunaraj, who was a favourite of Maharana Kumbha, built temples in Ajahari (Ajari), Pindarvataka (Pindwara)—both at present in the Sirohi territory—and Salera (Mewar) and renovated many old temples.[49]

Maharana Kumbha's treasurer Vela son of *Sah Kelá* built a temple at Chitor and dedicated it to Sāntinath.[50] Similarly, a Siva temple on a hill near the Sema village, not far from Eklingji, and several Jain temples in Vasantpur, Bhula and other places were built in Kumbha's time.

This shows that in Kumbha's time, Mewar was in a very prosperous condition and the people were rich and happy.

Singar Chanvri

Mid-way between the *Nava Lakha Bhandar* and the *Nava Kotha*, built by the imposter Banbir in A.D. 1537, and near the Tower of Victory, stands the 'graceful and richly carved'[51] building called the *Singar Chanvri* or *Vedi* built by Bhandari Velaka or Velā, son of Sah Kela, Maharana Kumbha's treasurer, in V.S. 1505 (A.D. 1448–49).

---

49. Bhavanagar Inscriptions, pp. 114–15.
50. Rajputana Museum Report for 1920–21, p. 5.
51. Cunninghan's *Archæological Survey Report*, Vol. XXIII, p. 118.

The building is square in plan with four wings projecting from its four sides and raised on a plinth some 5 feet in height. The main or central chamber of the Singar-Chanvri measure 22 feet internally both ways. Entrances are from the north and west, the sides east and south being filled by trellis windows. In the centre of this building, and raised 4 feet 1 inch from its floor, is a fortytwo-sided and highly ornamental *vedi*, or altar, which supports four carved pillars each 7 feet high and bearing lintels 1 foot 3 inches deep; thus the total height of the *vedi* is 8 feet 9 inches. This vedi is at present uncovered, save by the cupola of the temple itself, and the area between its pillars is 9 square feet. Along the edges of the *vedi*, run small water channels with outlets at the angles. The centre part of the building is covered by a circular Jain dome built in horizontal layers richly ornamented. The exterior walls are beautifully sculptured in horizontal bands containing numerous figures and floral scrobs and are worth study by any one who is a carver. The original roof terminations of the central chamber and porches of the building have disappeared. There is a perfect figure of Paraswanath over the west entrance and a less perfect one above the door to the north. Its architecture is admirable and the building, although small, is one of the most attractive in Chitor.

Sixteen

Kumbha as a Sovereign

Of the various Rajput clans, who have ruled or are ruling in Rajputana, only the Chauhans, the Guhilots (Sisodias) and the Rathods ever fought for the liberties of their country and played prominent parts in the history of Rajputana during the last 800 years. And of these three, the Chauhans of Ajmer alone achieved Imperial position, and became supreme rulers of India during the twelfth century of the Christian era. The Guhilots (Sisodias), after the decline of the Chauhans, achieved suzerain power in Rajputana and enjoyed a position, achieved by no other Rajput clan.

When the first Afghan invasion of India took place in A.D. 1191, it was the Chauhan Emperor Prithviraj who fought against the invader Shahbuddin Ghori. And later, when Babur invaded India, it was the Sisodia king, Maharana Sānga of Mewar, who, as the most powerful king of his time in India, headed the confederacy of the Rajput kings of Rajputana and well-versed in the *Smrities* (law), *Mimansa* (philosophy), *Natya Śastra* (Drama) *Rajaniti* (Political Science), *Ganita* (mathematics); *Vyakarana* (grammar), *Upanishads* (metaphysics) *Tarka* (logic) and *Sahitya* (general literature). He knew the Karnataki, the Maharashtri and other languages.

The commentary on *Gita Govinda*, named *Rasika Priya* and the last part of *Eklinga Mahatmya*, which was written during Kumbha's time, show that he was a great Sanskrit scholar, and that he wrote good poetry with as much ease as prose. The former work contains quotations from numerous Sanskrit works and shows that Kumbha was a man of extensive reading. The last part of *Eklinga Mahatmyá* is a lyric and its poetry is sweet and musical, and full of grace and beauty.

The *Eklinga Mahatmya*, sloka 74, mentions four dramas[2] written by him. This would show that he was a scholar of Prákrita, like the famous Chauhan Emperor Visaladeva; but, as none of his plays has so far been discovered, it is neither possible to speak of his proficiency in the Prákrita, nor to assign him a place due to him amongst the dramatists of India.

The *Kirtisthambha* Inscription, verse 158, says that in his four dramas he made use of Karnataki, Medapati and Mahárashtri languages, and adds that in *Nātaka* (play par excellence), *Prakarana* (play that takes a less elevated range than Nātaka) *Vithi* (one-act play performed by one or two actors) *Nātakā* (a play in four acts), *Bhán* (monologue in one act), *Prahasana* (farcical or comical satire in one act), *Rupaka* (drama generally) he was a new Bhārata.

---

2. Also Chitorgarh *Kirtisthambha* Inscription, V. 158.

KUMBHA AS A SCHOLAR 123

He was an accomplished musician and possessed a knowledge of the science, unequalled in his time. He was a most accomplished player on *Vina*, the noblest musical instrument invented by the Hindus. He was regarded as the highest authority on music; and because of this, the title of *Abhinava Bharátachárya* (new Bharatáchárya), as distinguished from the old Bharátachárya, the authority on *Natya Sastra* in ancient India, was conferred on him.[3]

His works[4] on the science of music, *Sangitarája*, *Sangita Mimánsá*, *Sudprabandha*, and *Rasika Priyá*[5] (commentary on the celebrated master piece, the lyric poem *Gita Govind*) and his commentary on *Sangita Ratnakar* are evidence of his mastery of the science. He composed numerous poetic invocations to gods to be sung in various *Rāgs* accompanied by different *Tāls*. They are to be found in the *Eklinga Māhatmya*.

Among other works known to have been written by him is a commentary on *Chandi Shataka*.[4]

Himself a great scholar, Maharana Kumbha always valued men of learning, and showed them respect and appreciated their work. The poets Atri, the composer of the first portion of the inscription on the Tower of Victory, and Mahesh, the composer of the remaining portion of it, lived in his court.

---

3. Kumbha's commentary on *Gita Govind*, p. 174. (Nirnayasagar Press, Bombay).
4. Chitorgarh *Kirtisthambha* Inscription, V. 157. See also Catalogue of Mss. Existing in the Central Provinces, by F. Keilhorn, Nagpur, A.D. 1874.
5. *Ibid*, V. 158.

He took great interest in architecture, as is clear from the magnificent buildings and works of art constructed during his time in Mewar—at Chitor, Abu, Kumbhalgarh, Ránpur and other places. A number of books on this noble art were written under his auspices, some of which have come to light. The following eight books on architecture and sculpture were written by Maharana Kumbha's architect Mandan,[6] son of Crikshetra (*vide* Abfrecht's Catalogus Catalogorum, Part I., pp. 730-1, Leipzic, A.D. 1891.

(1) देवतामूर्तिप्रकरण
(2) प्रासादमण्डन
(3) राजवल्लभ
(4) रूपमण्डन
(5) वास्तुमण्डन
(6) वास्तुशास्त्र
(7) वास्तुसार
(8) रूपावतार

Three other works on architecture by Mandan's son Govind, are:

उद्धारधोरणी, कलानिधि, द्वारदीपिका. Mandan's brother Natha, wrote वास्तुमंजरी. All these works are in existence at Udaipur and were seen with Champalal, a descendant of Manda, by Prof. S.R. Bhandarkar, as mentioned by him in his "Report of a second tour in search of Sanskrit manuscripts in Rajputana and Central India in A.D. 1905-6."

---

6. A copper-plate inscription of S. 1462 (A.D. 1405) in the possession of Champalal, a descendant of Mandana at Udaipur shows that Sutradhara Mandan was a native of Gujarat and had been brought to Udaipur by Maharana Mokal, father of Maharana Kumbha and granted a village for maintenance.

KUMBHA AS A SCHOLAR 125

Maharana Kumbhá had a work on the subject of *Kirtisthambha* (Tower of Fame or Victory), based on principles of Jaya and Aprajita written by one of his architects, and had it engraved on stone tablets and fixed in the lower part of the Tower of Victory. A part of the first tablet, found at Chitor and since deposited in the Udaipur Museum, says that the work was written under the orders of Maharana Kumbhá.

Fifteen

Inscriptions and Coins

INSCRIPTIONS

More than 60 inscriptions of the time of Maharana Kumbha have been discovered. The earliest inscription is dated the V.S. 1491 (A.D. 1434) and the latest, V.S. 1518 (A.D. 1461). Many of them are of the greatest importance to the history of India in general and of Rajputana in particular. They have thrown a flood of light on the history of Rajputana and elucidated several obscure points in the history of Mewar. It is due to the discovery and deciphering of some of these inscriptions that the splendid achievements of this great monarch have become known, and it has become possible to appreciate his elevated character, his great attainments, and his high position among the great monarchs of India. A few of these inscriptions are described below:—

1. The earliest stone inscription of the time of Maharana Kumbhā is that dated the *Kārtik Sud* 2, V.S. 1491 (A.D. 1434)

and is in the possession of *yati* Khemsāgar in the village Delwārā Udaipur State. It records that, during the victorious reign of Rana Kumbhakarna, 14 Tankas (silver coins) were allotted for the worship of Dharmachintāmani Temple as detailed below:—

5 Tankas from the Māndavi (custom house); 4 from the Mapa tax (octroi); 2 from Manahedavatā tax; 2 from Kharivata (Salt tax); and 1 from Patasuitriya (cloth tax) of Delwars.

This Inscription is published in Jainacharya Vijayadharmsuri's booklet *Deva Kulapātak*, p. 22.

2. Copper plate inscription of *Asādh Vad Amāvasyā*, S. 1494 (A.D. 1437) found in the village Nāndiya, (Sirohi State), and at present deposited in the Rajputana Museum, Ajmer. It records a grant of a well and land to one Prabhā Brahmin. (Unpublished).

3. Inscription of *Māgh Sud* 11, Thursday, S. 1494 (A.D. 1437) engraved on the pedestal of the magnificent image of Adhbudhji (Śāntinath) in the Jain temple of Adabadanāthji in the town of Nāgadā. It is transcribed in The *Bhāvanagar Inscriptions*, page 112. It records the erection of the image of Sāntināth by Sāh Sārang in the temple during the time of Maharna Kumbhā.

4. The celebrated Rānpur Temple Inscription of V.S. 1496 (A.D. 1439). This inscription and an English translation of it were first published by Peter Peterson in his *Bhāvanagar Inscriptions*. Dr. D.R. Bhandarkar, in his excellent article on the Rānpur Temple, contributed to the Annual Report of the Archæological Survey of India for 1907–8, re-translates the

inscription (p. 216). The inscription is engraved on a stone built up in a pillar to the left of the entrance into the Chaumukha Temple at Rānpur, about 6 miles from Sadadi in the Jodhpur State. The stone, a slab of white marble, measures 3 feet 3 inch by 1 feet 1 inch, and contains 47 lines of Sanskrit prose. It is well preserved. The inscription after stating that Sri Bappa was supreme ruler of Mewar in V.S. 1496, gives the genealogy of the Kings of Mewar up to Maharana Kumbhakaran, incidentally mentioning Rana Bhuvana Simh as the conqueror of Sultān Allauddin (Khilji) and the Chauhān king Kituka, and Rana Lakhshman Simh as the vanquisher of the king of Mālava (Malwa). Of Maharana Kumbhakaran, the inscription says:—

"The lion of the forest, *viz.*, (his) family, the king Rana Sri-Kumbhakarna, who had demonstrated the pride of the effulgence of a conqueror by seizing, in mere play, the several great fortresses (such as those) of the very inaccessible and impregnable Saramgapura, Nāgapura, Gagarana, Naranaka, Ajayameru, Mandora, Mandalakara, Bundi, Khatoo, Chatasoo, Jana, and others; who was like the lord of elephants, being exalted by his own *bhuja* (arms) and having acquired many *bhadras* (auspicious qualities, or elephants of a particular class); who was the lord of birds, i.e. Garuda, in having destroyed hoards of snake-like Mlechchha kings, whose foot-lotus was caressed by the rows of the foreheads of the kings of various countries, whose obstinate resistence was baffled by his terrible staff-like arm; who was a Govinda for his amorous dalliance with the faithful and lovely Lakshmi (goddess of sovereignty or the goddess Lakshmi); by the spreading of whose valour, which acted like wild fire to burn the thicket of bad polity, droves of beasts, *viz.*, all the powerful hostile kings, were fleeing away; whose title as the Hindu Sultān was proclaimed by the umbrella of royalty given (him) by the Sultans protecting Gurjaratra and the territory of Dhilli which were occupied by his great exploits; (who was) the asylum of the sacrifice of gold; who was the supporter of the duties (enjoined) in the six systems of philosophy; who was the ocean to the river, *viz.*, his quadripartite army; who imitated Sri-Rama, Yudhishthira, and other kings by his fame, virtue, protection of his subjects, truthfulness and other qualities."

5. A big stone inscription of *Māgh Sud 5*, V.S. 1500 (25th January, A.D. 1444), fixed in a wall in a temple of Krishna on a hill near the village of *Kadiyān* about 15 miles from Udaipur. It records that during the reign of Maharana Kumbhā, a Brahmin named Tilla Bhatta built the temple of Krishna. Tilla Bhatta is stated to have belonged to the Bharadwaja Gotra and his two predecessors were Sihad and Villa Bhatta. Tilla Bhatta had received honours from Maharana Kumbha. (Unpublished).

6. *Rupāheli Inscription*—An inscription engraved on the back of a Jain image in the Jain temple at Rupāheli (Mewar). It is dated the 1st day of the dark half of *Ashādha*, Samvat 1505 (A.D. 1448) and records that the image was set up by Sā (Saha) Sāliga, his wife Hansu, their son Narasinha, his wife Jivani, their son Israna and his wife Lisi; all belonging to the Ukesa (Oswāl) family and Malya Gotra. See Report of the Rajputana Museum, Ajmer, for A.D. 1926, p. 2.

7. Four inscriptions dated the full moon day of the bright half of *Mārga* (Margasirsha), Sam. 1505 (A.D. 1448) recording

the installation of the images of Sridhara, Krishna-Rukmini, Rama-Lakhmana and Madhava-Tulasi by Maharana Kumbhakarna of Mewar. The inscriptions are engraved on the pedestals of the images which are placed in the niches of the Mandapa of the temple of Kumbhasvami at Chitor. *Vide*, The Rajputana Museum Report for 1917–18, p. 2.

8. An Inscription engraved on a pillar in the temple, known as *Singār Chanvri* at Chitor. It is dated Samvat 1505 (A.D. 1448). It refers to "the time of Rana Kumbhakarna (Kumbha), son of Rana Mokal, son of Rana Lakha." It records the erection of a temple of the Jain *Tirthankara* Santinatha by Bhandari Velaka, son of Saha Kelha, the treasurer of Rana Kumbhakarna (Kumbha). It mentions Velaka's wives Vilhanadē and Ratnadē, and his sons Mundharaja, Dhanaraja and Kumarapala. The consecration was performed by Jinasenasuri of the Kharataragachchha. It also mentions the names of the Jain pontiffs Jiraraja, Jinavardhana, Jinachandra, Jinasagara and Jinasundarasuri in order of succession. Pandit Udayasilagani is also mentioned as paying his obeisance. See Rajputana Museum Report for 1920–21, p. 5.

9. Inscription of *Asādh Sud* 2, S. 1506 (A.D. 1449) engraved on a pillar in the courtyard between the famous temples of Vimal Shah and Tejpāl at Abu. It records the abolition, at the request of the Maharana's minister Dunger Bhoja, of the Pilgrim tax, Customs, *Valhavi* (armed escort) and Chaukidari and Cattle taxes levied in Abu in those days. This inscription is published in the *Nāgari Prachārīnī Patrikā*, New Series, Vol. I, p. 450–51.

10. An inscription on a perforated stone window in the second storey of the *Kīrtisthambhā* (Tower of Victory) of

Maharana Kumbha at Chitor. It is dated the 5th day of the bright half of *Phālguna*, Samvat 1499 (A.D. 1443). It belongs to the reign of Maharajadhiraja Maharana Kumbhakarna (Kumbha) and records the offering of obeisance to god Samiddhesva (Samiddhesvara) by Sutradhara (architect) Ja-i-ta (Jaita) and his two sons Nāpā and Punjā. (Unpublished).

11. An inscription engraved on the pedestal of a Jain image lying in the Jain temple at Vasantgarh in the Sirohi State. The inscription is greatly defaced. It is of the reign of Maharana Kumbhakarna of Mewar and is dated Wednesday, the 11th day of the bright half of *Māgh*, Samvat 1507 (A.D. 1450). It states that the image was set up in the Vasantpura Chaitya (temple) by Bhadaka, son of Dhansi and others, and was consecrated by Muni Sundersuri. *Vide*, Rajputana Museum Report for 1924, pp. 3-4.

12-15. Four inscriptions engraved on the pedestals of the images of Vasudeva, Damodar etc. in Kumbhalgarh, all dated *Asoj Sud* 3rd, S. 1516 (A.D. 1459) recording the erection of the images of Vasudeva etc. by Maharana Kumbha. All these inscriptions are deposited in the Udaipur Museum.

16. The famous Kumbhalgarh inscription of *Magsar Bad* 5, V. S. 1517 (A.D. 1460) in the Mamādeva (Kumbhasvami) temple. This inscription was engraved on five big slabs, of which the first, third and fourth slabs and a small part of the second, are deposited in the Victoria Hall Museum at Udaipur. The fifth and the greater part of the second slab have disappeared. The first slab contains 64 slokas, and gives an account of the temples, lakes and sacred places of Mewar. The third gives the traditional accounts of Bappa Rawal and others.

Sloka 138 says: "An account of *Rājvamsa* (Rulers of Mewar) based on several inscriptions is here given." It gives an account of the geneology of the kings of Mewar from Guhil to Rāwal Ratna Singh and an account of Lakhshman Singh of Sisodā.

The fourth slab records that Maharana Lakhamsi went to Heaven with his seven sons, while fighting with the Mussalmāns (Allāuddin Khilji). In his family was born Arisimha who was like Narasimha and pierced the temples of the elephants of his enemies with his sword. He (Arisimha) was succeeded by his son Hammira, who was very liberal and brave. He conquered the fortress called Chelvāta (Jilwara). He was succeded by his son Kshetrasimha, who defeated the army of the Yavanas near Chitor. He defeated Dafar Khan (Zafar Khān), the lord of Pattan (Patan, *i.e.* Gujarat), Ami Shah (Dilawar Khān Ghori of Malwa, *vide*, *Memoirs of Jehangir* by Alexander Rogers, Vol. I, page 407, and Elliot's *History of India*, Vol. IV, page 552) and imprisoned Ranamalla (Raja of Idar). He conquered the rulers of Hādāvati (Hārāvati), brought their country under his control and destroyed their fortress of Mandalakara (Māndalagarh). He also defeated the ruler of Malwa several times and imprisoned the rulers of Gujarāt. His son was Lakshasena (Lakhamansimha, Lākhā), who weighed himself against gold and liberated Tristhali (Kāsi, Prayāga and Gayā) from the Sakas (Musalmans). He defeated the Medas (Mers) and took from them the mountain Vardhana (fortress of Badnor). His son was Mokalendra, who made those Brahmans, who had become cultivators, study Vedas, and weighed himself against gold. He conquered the whole country of Sapādalaksha and took Sākamabhari (Sāmbhar). He defeated Peroz (Firoz Khan of Nagor), Muhammad (Ahmad Shāh of Gujarat) and destroyed their elephants. He repaired the temple of Samiddhesvara at Chitor and also built the holy places known as Ranamochana, Pāpamochana and a beautiful reservoir. He set up in the temple of *devi*, a lion made of all the metals and presented a gold Garuda (eagle) to the temple of Vishnu. His son was Kumbhakarna, whose mother was Sobhagyadevi. He rebuilt the ruined temple of Eklinga and adorned it with golden *kalasas*. He was clever in composing poems and fearless in battles. He was a jewel of the family of Guhadatta, Khomana, Śalivāhana, Ajaya, Kshetra, Laksha and Mokal. He subjugated the ruler of the town called Nāradiya, conquered Yoginipura, (Jāwar), humbled the pride of the ruler of Sodhyā and took possession of Mandovara (Mandor). He captured Hammirapur from Ranavira, destroyed Dhanyanagara and conquered Yagapura (Jahazpur). He placed his left foot on the head of the brave lord of Mālava (Malwa) and took Janakāchal. He defeated the ruler of Vrindavati (Bundi), burnt his town and captured the fortress of Gargarata (Gagroon). He burnt Mallaranyapur (Malarna), wrested Simhapuri (Sihor), destroyed Ratnapura and imprisoned several rulers. He overran the country of Sapadalaksha, conquered Ranasthambha (Ranthambhor), Amradadri (Amber), Kotra and Bombaovada, and captured the fortress of Mandalgarh. He conquered several countries and fortresses, subjugated the rulers of Hārāvati and exacted tribute from them. He devastated Visalanagara, conquered Giripura (Dungarpur) and put its ruler Gayapala to flight. He humbled the pride of the Muhammadans at Sārangapur and imprisoned several young women of the Lord of Pārasikas (Muhammadans).

134 MAHARANA KUMBHA

The unfortunate loss of the fifth slab renders the account of Maharana Kumbha incomplete. The fact that some of the slokas are common to this and the Chitor *Kirtisthambha* Inscription (no. 14 below), as also the fact that both bear the same date, show that both of them were composed by the same poet. This inscription gives a more detailed account of Kumbha, while the Chitor *Kīrtisthambha* Inscription is brief. These two are the most important of all inscriptions of Kumbha's time.

17. The Chitor *Kīrtisthambha* (Tower of Victory) Inscription of *Magsar Bad* 5th, S. 1517 (A.D. 1460). It was engraved on several stone slabs, of which only two are now in existence, first and the last but one, containing slokas 1 to 28 and 168 to 187, respectively. A photo transcript of these two slabs is published in Cunningham's Archæological Survey Report), Vol. 23, Plates 20 and 21. Several more slabs were in existence in A.D. 1678, when a Pundit copied the inscription engraved on them, in a book of 22 leaves on *Fagan Bad* 7th, S. 1735 (A.D.1678). This copy is in Mahamahopadhyaya P. Gauri Shankar's possession. The first two verses are devoted to the praise of Siva and Ganesa. The description of the family of Bappa commences from verse 3. Verses 4–8 are devoted to Bappa who is said to have been a great warrior, a leader of the princes and a devotee of Siva. In his family was born, Hammir who destroyed his enemies. He was very liberal and was called Vishamdhāti Panchānana (a lion in vigorous attacks). He captured his enemy's fortress Chelvāta (Jilwārā) (verses 9–20). His son was Kshetrasinha who destroyed the army of the Yavanas (Ami Shāh, *alias* Dilāwar Khān Ghori of Mālwā) near Chitor and imprisoned

Ranamalla of Idar (verses 21-29). His son was Lakshasinh who liberated Gayā from the Muhammadans. He weighed himself against gold and captured Vardhamanagiri (Badnor) from the Mevas (Mers; verses 30-39). His son was Mokal (V. 40).

After this, 193 verses are devoted to the description of Rana Kumbhakarna's reign and the number of the verses again begins with one.

Rana Kumbha brought the image of Hanuman from Māndavyapura (Mandor) and established it in the fortress of Kumbhalgarh. He exacted tribute from the country of Sapādalaksha (Sāmbhar) and brought from there the image of Umā. He levied taxes from the salt mines at Dindvana (Didwana in Jodhpur State), took the town of Naraina (in Jaipur State) and conquered the whole kingdom of Mudafar (Muzaffar Shah). He re-populated the town of Vasantapur near the holy fountain of Vasishtha (*i.e.* Mt. Abu) and built there seven tanks. He built to the east of the temple of Eklinga, a Mandapa known as Kumbhamandapa. He with his cavalry attacked Gokarnagiri and the kingdom of Arbuda (Mt. Abu), on the peak of which he built the fortress of Achaldurga (Achalgarh); he erected there the grand Vishnu temple of Kumbhasvámi, and near it, built a tank. This crest-jewel of kings built four other tanks on Mount Abu. He subjugated Muhammad, destroyed the town of Nagapur (Nagor) with the lofty *mashiti* (masjid), built by Peroz (Firoz), imprisoned several young Muhammadan women and took possession of the treasure of Shams Khan while fighting in the country of Jāngal. He laid waste Khandela and erected the lofty temple of Kumbhaswami at Chitor. Near it, he also erected another temple of Adivarāha, dug a tank called Ramakund, erected the lofty *Kirtisthambha* and constructed a road for chariots from the bottom of the fort to its top. At Chitor, he constructed Rāmarathyā (Rampol gate), Hanumanagopura (Hanumanpol), Bhairavankavisikha (Bhairavapol), Mahalakshmirathyā (Mahalakshmipol), Chāmundapratoli (Chamundapol), and Tararathyā (Tarapol; VV. 1–42).

(Verses 43–124 were missing even at that time, A.D. 1678).

He (Kumbhakarna) built Rājapratoli (Rājpol=the palace gate) with an ornamental *Torana* (V. 125). He built the fortress of Kumbhalmeru (Kumbhalgarh) with four gates on the top of Vindya mountain, constructed there the temple of Kumbhasvāmi in honour of Vishnu, and near it, built a beautiful lake. On the top of the fortress, he set up the image of Ganésa brought from one of his enemies's fortresses. (VV. 126–146). He was called Rājguru, Dānaguru, Śailaguru and Paramaguru of Kings. He killed several of his enemies to take revenge of his father's death. He was versed in the four Vedas, composed Sangitarāja, Sūdaprabandha and four dramas. He wrote commentaries on *Chandishataka* and *Gīta Govinda*. He was the head of poets, princes, and skilled in playing on the lute (*vinā*). In dramatic composition, he was a Bharat and followed the rules, of Nandikesvara, while composing poems in praise of Siva. He destroyed the combined armies of the lords of Mālwā and Gujarat in war and captured several elephants. He assumed the titles, Asvapati, Gajapati and Narapati. He was the son of Sobhāgyadevi, and husband of Kumbhaladevi. He built a new Visikhā (gate) on the 13th day of the dark half of *Kārtika*, Samvat 1507; Kumbhalmeru on the 13th day of the dark half of *Chaitra*, Samvat 1515; *Kirtisthambha* on the 10th day of the bright half of *Māgha*, Samvat 1505, and Achaldurga on the 15th day of the bright half of *Māgha*, Samvat 1509. (VV. 147-187).

In the family of Bhrigu was born Somnāth. His son was Narahari whose son was Kesáva also called Jhoting. Jhoting's son was Atri, who composed a part of the *Prasasti*. His son Mahesh, who was highly honoured by Kumbhakarna, completed the *Prasasti* on Monday the 5th day of the dark half of *Mārgasirsha*, Samvat 1517 (A.D. 1460).

18. The second Kumbhalgarh Inscription of *Magsar Bad 5*, Monday) V.S. 1517 (A.D. 1460). Of this inscription, the first slab containing 64 slokas, alone remains: the remaining slabs are lost. The first slab contains a part of an account of Maharana Kumbha. It says that the account is continued in subsequent slabs. The slab is in the Museum at Udaipur. (Unpublished).

19. Inscription dated the *Vaisakh Sud* 4th, V.S. 1518 (A.D. 1461) engraved on the pedestal of the magnificent brass image of Adinātha in the Achalgarh Jain temple at Abu. It records that while Maharajadhiraja Kumbhakarana was ruling at Kumbhalmeru, the image was made at Dungarpur during the reign of Rāwal Somadāsa and brought to Abu by the Sangha (community) of Tapagachchha. It was set up by Sā Sābha, his wife Karanādé and their sons Sālā and Mālā. The consecration ceremony was performed by Lakshmisāgarasuri of Tapagachcha.

COINS

Maharana Kumbhā struck gold, silver and copper coins *Ferishta* (Briggs' Translation, Vol. IV, page 221) mentions gold coins of Kumbhā. In the Mamādeva temple in the fort of Kumbhalgarh, there is an image, of the size of a man, of *Kuvér*, treasurer of the gods, with two attendants pouring coins from bags into plates. One plate is full of circular coins and the other square ones, which shows that Maharana Kumbha's coins were of two varieties, circular and rectangular. The coins that have come to light so far are only copper ones. They are of five kinds, all square or rectangular in shape. The Obverse contains the name of Maharana Kumbhakaran, and the Reverse either Kumbhalmeru or Eklingji. The biggest of them, has the year V.S. 1517 (A.D. 1460).

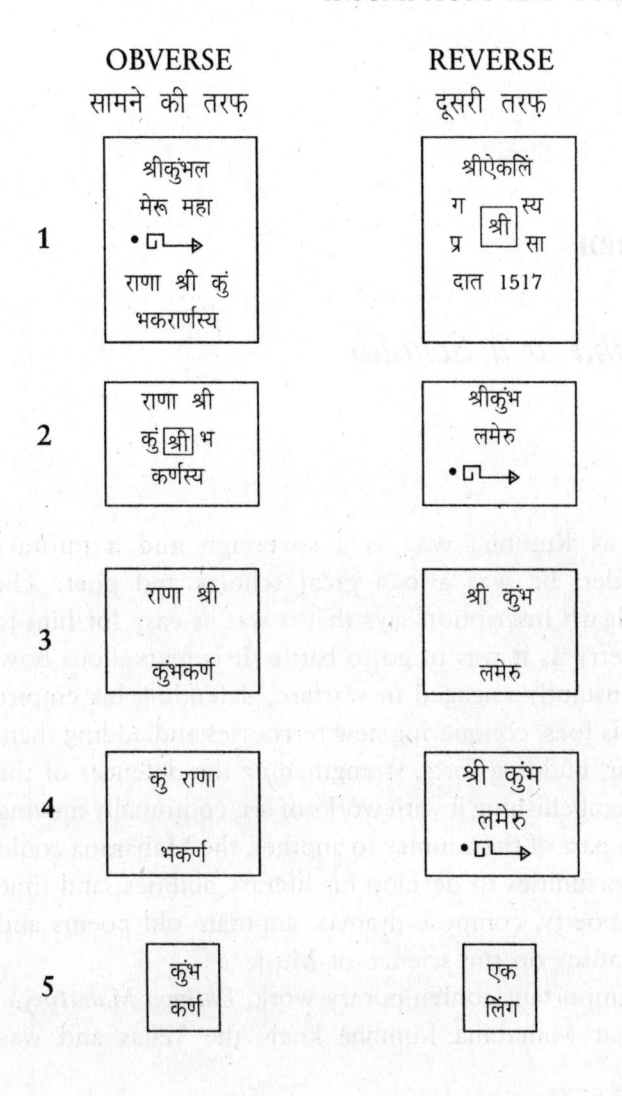

INSCRIPTIONS AND COINS 139

	OBVERSE सामने की तरफ़	REVERSE दूसरी तरफ़
1	श्रीकुंभल मेरू महा • ⌐→ राणा श्री कुं भकरार्णस्य	श्रीऐकलिं ग ┌─┐ स्य प्र │श्री│ सा └─┘ दात 1517
2	राणा श्री कुं [श्री] भ कर्णस्य	श्रीकुंभ लमेरु • ⌐→
3	राणा श्री कुंभकर्ण	श्री कुंभ लमेरु
4	कुं राणा भकर्ण	श्री कुंभ लमेरु • ⌐→
5	कुंभ कर्ण	एक लिंग

Fourteen

Kumbha as a Scholar

Great as Kumbhá was as a sovereign and a military commander, he was also a great scholar and poet. The Kumbhalgarh Inscription says that it was as easy for him to write poetry as it was to go to battle. It is marvellous how, while constantly engaged in warfare, defending his empire against his foes, conquering new territories and adding them to Mewar, building forts, strengthening the defences of the country, embellishing it with works of art, continually moving from one part of the country to another, the Maharana could find opportunities to develop his literary abilities, and time to write poetry, compose dramas, annotate old poems and write treatises on the science of Music.

The important contemporary work, *Eklinga Mahatmya*[1] shows that Maharana Kumbhā knew the Vedas and was

---

1. *Eklinga Mahatamya*, Rajvaran Adhyay, slokas 172–73.

KUMBHA AS A SOVEREIGN

the Pathan Sultan of Delhi, and opposed the Turk invader. Thus, the Chauhans as the Imperial Power in India, and the Guhilot Maharana of Chitor as the suzerain power in Rajputana, led the opposition, when the Afghans and the Turks first came to conquer India.

The Rathods came to Rajputana in the thirteenth century A.D. and rapidly spread in its western parts. They had several times to fight against the Afghan Sultans and Turk Emperors of Delhi in defence of their country, and materially helped in bringing about the fall of the Turk empire in India.

The Kachhwāhas of Jaipur were minor chieftains till the middle of the sixteenth century, and only came into prominence under Raja Bhagvandas in Akbar's time. They were the first amongst the Rajputs to accept Turk suzerainty: and they never took up arms against the Emperors of Delhi.

While the Rathods, and sometimes the Deoras (Chauhans) of Sirohi, fought against the Turk emperors of Delhi, it was the Maharanas of Mewar, who continually opposed the Turks, never bowing their head to them. They sacrificed their all to preserve their independence and self respect. Maharana Kumbha was not only one of the greatest of the Maharanas, but was the real founder of the greatness of Mewar.

Maharana Kumbha reigned from A.D. 1433 to A.D. 1468. The period marks the consolidation of the power of Mewar, which under the great Hindupati Maharana Sanga and the immortal Pratap, shone so brilliantly in the following century when the great adventurer from Samarkand invaded India, and his grandson Akbar, the greatest of the Mughal emperors of India, founded a magnificent empire in this country. The period also marks the rise of the Rathod Power, which later becoming famous in history as the *Lākh Talwar Rathodān*, played a prominent part in the foundation and the consolidation of the Mughal Empire during the reigns of Akbar, Jahangir and Shah Jahan; and which eventually helped in giving the death stroke to that empire during the time of Aurangzeb and his successors. The popular couplet:

हथनापुर हलचल मची, पड़ी सितारे गल्ल।
धुंवां आंबर ढाकया वै रूठा रिड़मल्ल॥

"There is consternation in Delhi; anxiety prevails in Satara (amongst Marhattas). The sky has become overcast with gloom; for, the Rathods have been offended."

illustrates the power, the Rathods wielded in India during the 18th century.

Maharana Kumbha, was a great sovereign, a great military commander, a great builder and a great scholar. Rarely has the world seen such a combination of qualities in one man, each of which would stamp a man, great. It is wonderful how a great sovereign like Maharana Kumbha, constantly engaged in warfare from almost his childhood, could find time and opportunities to become a great poet and dramatist, a master of the science of music, and write commentaries on *Gita Govind*—one of the master-pieces of lyric literature in the world—and books like *Chandi Shataka* and *Sangit Ratnakar*, and a treatise on the architectural art of building Towers of Victory (*Kirtisthambha*). Contemporary European history does not furnish an example of a great monarch who was also a great administrator, a great general, a great builder, a great poet, and a great author. India, with its great historic past, the home of religion, science and philosophy, where great ethical truths and cultural traditions have so deeply permeated the life of the common people, has been in a favourable position to give to the world great men.

Amongst the Rajput sovereigns of Rajputana, Kumbha occupies a most prominent position. His natural abilities and his achievements place him in the forefront among the great rulers not only of Mewar, but of the whole of India. The best known Maharanas of Mewar are Maharana Sānga, Maharana Pratap and Maharana Raj Singh. Now, Maharana Pratap stands by himself. He is beyond compare. He lived in times so different from those of Kumbha or Sanga, that no comparison between him and the other Maharanas is possible. Pratap had, as his enemy, one of the greatest sovereign of all times in Asia or Europe, and had had ranged against him not only the whole might of Akbar's Empire, but also the knowledge and resources of the kings of Amber (Jaipur), Jodhpur and Bikaner. Yet, he triumphed over this powerful combination and succeeded in preserving the independence of Mewar and the liberties of his people.

For sheer intellectual ability, however, Kumbha takes the first place amongst the Maharanas of Mewar. If we consider his great work for the defences and the embellishment of Mewar, he again stands easily the first. As an ever-victorious monarch, he stands unrivalled amongst the kings of India of the last thousand years.

Sāngā also was a great sovereign, and triumphed over all his enemies except Babur. Maharana Raj Singh had to fight the Moghal Empire in India at its zenith, and succeeded in defeating the attempts of Aurangzeb to reduce Mewar to submission. But the heroic and successful fights the Maharanas were able to put up against the Moghal Emperors were in no small measure due to the immensely strengthened defences of Mewar, effected by the foresight and wisdom of Maharana Kumbha.

Kumbha was in every respect, the equal of Sāngā, and in some respects, his superior. If Kumbha or Sānga's elder brother Prithviraj, had been in Sānga's place to lead the Indian opposition to Babur, Babur would, in all probability, have ended his days in Kabul. If Kumbhā is not so well-known to readers of history, it is because important Persian histories which began to be written only with the advent of the Moghals (Turks) in India have given little attention to events that occurred before Babur came to this country. And the English histories, which are based entirely on Persian histories, only repeat what the latter have recorded. Sāngā's fame rests chiefly on the accounts given of his character and his exploits by the memoirs of Babur and Humayun, and the histories written by writers who hovered round the Moghal Court. Kumbha has not had that advantage.

The Rajputs had produced men as great and as remarkable as Kumbha, before the latter appeared on the scene. The great Chauhan Emperor Visaldeva,[1] the uncle of the famous Emperor Prithviraj, who flourished in the 12th century of the

---

1. For an account of Emperor Visaldeva, see my article on him in the *Vedic Magazine and Gurukul Samachar* of Aswin, V.S. 1969, Vol. IV, pp. 292–97, and my book, *Ajmer: Historical and Descriptive*, page 154.

Christian era, besides being a great sovereign and a great military commander, was also a great scholar. He conquered the whole of Upper India, carried his arms right up to the Himalayas, making Delhi a tributary to Ajmer, which then became the capital of the Indian Empire. In his inscription on the famous Siwalik Pillar, originally erected in Gurhwal by Emperor Asoka—who according to H.W. Wells, the author of the *Outline of History*, is the greatest monarch of all times—and which now stands in the *Firozshah ka Kotla* at Delhi, Emperor Visaldeva states that he had freed Hindustan of all invaders from the North-West. He was not only a great king and a great commander, but also a scholar and a dramatist, as is proved by his drama *Harkeli Nātak*, parts of which engraved on black basalt slabs, are preserved in the Rajputana Museum, Ajmer.

The great Parmār sovereign, Raja Bhoja of Dhārānagiri, who flourished in the eleventh century of the Christian era was a great general, a great scholar and a great sovereign.[2]

Three great personalities emerge from the events that

---

2. The eminent orientalist, K.P. Jayaswal, in his article on the Udaipur temple of Malwa in the *Modern Review* for June, 1932, p. 604, says about Raja Bhoja:—
 "The most famous king of the eleventh century in India was Bhoja of the Parmār dynasty, who was king of Malwa from A.D. 1010 to 1050 His undertakings were gigantic: he surveyed the whole of Sanskrit and Prakrit literature and had encyclopædias on art and sciences compiled, books on literary art criticism written, vast anthologies prepared, books on the art of poetics, on astrology, astronomy, music and architecture composed, and Hindu law re-stated. In this survey of national culture, be took part personally

crowd the life of the first half of the fifteenth century of the history of Mewar. The dominating personality of the period was the great Maharana Kumbha. During his time, two other remarkable men appeared on the scene: 1. Rao Chondā, the founder of the House of Saloombar and progenitor of the Chondawats of Mewar; who in his life, illustrated qualities,

---

more than what Napolean did in the preparation of Code Napoleon. Bhoja was one of the greatest scholars of his time, he had his own theories on poetics. He was a very keen art-critic, and composed very fine verses extempore.

"In the domain of kingship, he was the best general of his time. As in Napoleon so in Bhoja, literary taste and soldierly ability were united. In the history of Hindu law, Bhoja is a landmark: with him the Mitakshara law, which reigns to-day, arose. As an architect and builder, Bhoka was one of the greatest men. He conceived the idea of turning the parched hills of the Vindhayas in Malwa into a green paradise and succeeded in doing so. His lake which, on expert calculation, covered 260 square miles, changed the climate of Malwa. In Muhammadan times when the lake was still existing, there came into vogue the saying, 'I wish, I enjoyed the night of Malwa and the morning of Benares. The nights of Malwa have ceased to be of that charm with the destruction of the lake. The lake was named 'Bhojapala; *pal*, in the language of Malwa, even to-day means the embankment of an artificial lake. Bhoja-pal is now pronounced as Bho-pal."

The well-known Hindi couplet

ताल तो भोपाल ताल और सब तलइयां हैं।

गढ़ तो चित्तोड़ गढ़ और सब गढ़इयां हैं ॥

"Lakes: There is only one lake, the Bhopal lake; others are ponds of water. Chitorgarh is the only fort; others are mere fortified places," shows that the people held the Bhopal lake to be the king of the lakes of the world.

that illumine history and ennoble Rajput traditions; and 2. Rao Rān Mal of Mandor, whose son Jodha founded Jodhpur and laid the foundations of the Rathod Power, which during the later Mughals was one of the principal forces to be reckoned with in Indian history.

Great as Kumbha was, Rao Chondā also was a remarkable man. His nobility of mind and chivalrous character not only distinguish him from the ordinary run of chieftains in Rajputana, but have placed him amongst the noblest of Rajputs in India. Like Sri Ram Chandra of Ayodhya, one of the noblest of mortal men, and, according to the Hindus, 'the perfect man,' Chondā, springing from the same noble stock, *Raghuvamsa*, has given to the world an example of a life of high spiritual elevation and moral grandeur, rare in human annals.

Rao Rān Mal of Mandor, who also, out of filial love and obedience, gave up his right to the throne of Mandor, and who, inspite of the unjust treatment meted out to him, always showed during his exile, the same respect to his father, and devotion to the interests of his country as before, was a remarkable man of great mortal worth. Physically a giant amongst men, a great general, and a man of immense energy and resource and of great courage, he repaid a thousand fold to Mewar, the debt he owed to Maharama Mokal, by rendering her services which a true student of history must acknowledge with admiration. His achievements are a source of pride to all who call themselves Rathods.

While we pay homage to the greatness of Maharana Kumbha, and have great reverence and respect for Rawat Chondā, and admiration and esteem for Rao Rān Mal, the thought obtrudes itself as to why notwithstanding the possession of the noble qualities with which nature richly endowed him, Kumbha, who was ever successful in all his undertakings—successful not only in defending his kingdom against the united efforts of the most powerful kings of his time; successful in punishing the enemies of his country and his religion—failed to restore Rajput supremacy in Upper India, and free Western India from the tyranny and the domination of the Afghan adventurers who had usurped supreme power in some of those parts, by crushing once for all his enemies, eminently fitted as he was to do so.

The answer is writ large on every page of Indian history. The Hindus had, owing to various causes, the principal one being the rise amongst them of certain schools of religious thought, lost the one quality necessary to achieve political success. Maharana Kumbha, and after him, Maharana Sanga, both failed to save India from being subjected to foreign domination, because of the lack of that quality. That quality is *political foresight*, which comes only of full *national consciousness*.

The introduction of the caste system in the social polity of the Hindus cut up the nation into a number of parts, each part becoming, as time progressed, more and more conscious of its separateness from the other parts, and sapped the foundations of a common nationality and destroyed national consciousness among the Hindus.

Historical and other records show that the Hindus long before the earliest invasions from the North-West began to take place, had, owing to their acceptance of certain moral and spiritual principles of life ceased to be an aggressive race.

KUMBHA AS A SOVEREIGN 149

The wish to dominate other people for their economic exploitation or, to impose their rule in order to force their religious beliefs on the subject races, has always been absent from their character. They never thought of invading their neighbours' countries like Mahmud Ghaznavi, Shahbuddin Ghori, Timur, or Changez Khan. Live and let live, has been their rule of life, due to the teachings of their religion and philosophy, which have influenced their lives more than has been the case with other peoples.

During the last two thousand years and more, the Hindus have confined their political activities to defending themselves and their possessions when attacked by others. After the rise of those schools of thought, of which the doctrine of *Ahimsa* was a cardinal feature, and which produced repercussions on the social organisation of the people dividing them into watertight compartments, the Hindus as a nation, lost thought of *national* preservation and national well-being, and gave themselves up to practices which they thought, would secure them individual salvation. With their neglect of *politics*, they not only ceased to grow and to be self-assertive, but ceased even to take necessary precautions to preserve their national independence, and protect their country and their liberties from foreign invasion. It became their belief that it was inconsistent with the teachings of their religion and the high principles of their moral philosophy, to attack their neighbours and crush them when they could easily do so, even though this was necessary to save their country from attack. They even went further, and, as we have seen in this book, spared their foes when the latter fell into their hands, and sometimes even sent them home loaded with gifts under proper escort, completely ignoring the direful results of similar previous acts of mis-conceived generosity, repeatedly shown by Hindu monarchs.

They never learnt the lesson that the best defence against an enemy is to attack him, and that one can never break the power of an enemy by limiting one's activities to mere defence. The inevitable result of a purely defensive policy is loss of one's possessions. The law of nature is that you must advance, make progress or fall back and disappear. Individuals may comfort themselves that they would gain Heaven by pursuing this policy, but they would lose their freedom and their country as surely as that the day follows the night.

It is the first principle of political conduct that you should not only defend yourself against attack but should, if possible, break the power of your enemy by attacking him and rendering him incapable of doing you harm. Help the weak by all means, do justice to all but also do justice to yourself and to those who depend on you and whom, it is your duty, so far as possible, to protect from present or future attacks. Depriving enemies of the power of doing you harm is doing nothing more than protecting yourself. Failure to do so, whether in obedience to teachings of false philosophy, or owing to indolence or weakness, is failure to do your duty. The adoption by the Hindus of the foolish and futile policy of limiting their activities to defending themselves when attacked, resulted in their subjugation in the 12th and the 16th centuries A.D.; for they had failed to learn the lesson that history teaches to all nations, and Indian history so emphatically, to the Hindus.

Appendix

Shringirishi Inscription, dated *Sawan Sud 5*, V.S. 1485 (17th July, A.D. 1428)

आजावमीसाहमसिप्रभावाज्जित्वा च हत्वा यवनानशेषान्।
यः कोशजातं तुरगानसंख्यान्समानयत्स्वां किल राजधानीं ॥6॥
ढिल्ली चारुपुरेश्वरेण व(ब)लिना सृष्टोऽपि नो पाणिना
राज्ञा श्रीमददावदीति विलसन्नाम्ना गजस्वामिना।
सोपि क्षेत्रमहीभुजा निजभुजप्रौढप्रतापादहो
भग्नो विश्रुतमणडलाकृतिगढो जित्वा समसतानरीन् ॥7॥
दत्वा...तुरंगंहेमनिचयास्तस्मै ग...स्वामिने
मुक्ता येन कृता गयाकरभराद्धर्षणयनेकान्यतः।
प्रीताः स्वर्गगता वदंति पितरः स्वद्यापि सत्याशिषं
तस्या सा वि...क्ष भूतले भुजो वंशश्विरं नंदतु ॥11॥
यस्याग्रे समभूतपलायनप...पेरोजखानास्वयं
पात्साहोह्लाददुः महोपि समरे संत्यज्यको...।
त्राणवशेन शुष्कवदनो मुक्तालकारुद्वा

गश्वेनापि विवर्जितो गिरिगुहा गेहाश्रितः सांप्रतं ॥14॥
येन स्फाटिकसच्छिलामय इव ख्यातो महीमंडले
प्राकारो रचितः सुधाधवलितो देवैकलिं... ।
......सत्कपाटविलसद्द्वारत्रयालंकृतः
कैलासं तु विहाय शुंभुरकरोद्यत्राधिवासे मतिं ॥16॥

II

The Samiddeshwar (Mokalji) Temple Inscription (Chitor) dated *Magh Sudh* 3rd V.S. 1485 (A.D. 1429).

नेता पातोत्तराशा यवननरपतिं लुंठितारोषसेनं
पीरोजं कीर्तिवध्वीकुसुममुरुपतिं यो करोत्संगरस्थः ।
पल्लोशाक्रान्तितवार्तां कलयति कलयाकीर्त्तितां यस्य हेलां
पंचास्यस्येव माघदुगाजदलनरुचेलीलया रंकुभंगं ॥51॥

III

Rānpur *Chaumukha* Temple Inscription, dated V.S. 1496 (A.D. 1439).

स्वस्ति श्रीचतुर्मुखजिनयुगादीश्वराय नमः॥ श्रीमद्विक्रमतः 1496 संख्यवर्षे श्रीमेदापाटराजाधिराजश्रीबप्प 1 श्रीगुहिल 2 भोज 3 शील 4 कालभोज 5 भर्तृभट 6 सिंह 7 महायक 8 राझीसुतयुतस्वसुवर्ण तुलातोलकश्रीखुम्माण 9 श्रीमदल्लट 10 नरवाहन 11 शक्तिकुमार 12 शुचिवर्म 13 कीर्तिवर्म 14 योगराज 15 वैरट 16 वंशपाल 17 वैरीसिंह 18 वीरसिंह 19 श्रीअरिसिंह 20 चोडसिंह 21 विक्रमसिंह 22 रणसिंह 23 खेमसिंह 24 सामंतसिंह 25 कुमारसिंह 26 मथनसिंह 27 पदमसिंह 28 जैत्रसिंह 29 तेजस्वीसिंह 30 समरसिंह 31 चाहुमानश्रीकीतूकनृप-

श्रीआल्लावदीनसुरत्राणजैत्रबप्पवंश्यश्रीभुवनसिंह 32 सुतश्रीजयसिंह 33 मालवेशगोगादेवजैत्रश्रीलक्ष्मसिंह 34 पुत्रश्रीअजयसिंह 35 भ्रातृश्रीअरिसिंह 36 श्रीहम्मीर 37 श्रीखेतासिंह 38 श्रीलक्षाह्ययनरेन्द्र 39 नन्दनसुवर्णतुलादिदानपुण्य-परोपकारादिसारगुणसुरद्रुमविश्रामनन्दनश्रीमोकलमहीपति 40 कुलकाननपञ्चाननस्य विषमतमाभङ्गसारङ्गपुरनागपुरगागरणनराणाकाऽजयमेरुमण्डोरमण्डलकरबुदीखाटूचाटसूजानादिनानामहा दुर्गलीलामात्रग्रहणप्रमाणितजितकाशित्वाभिमानस्य निजभुजोर्जितसमुपार्जितानेकभद्रगजेन्द्रस्य म्लेच्छमहीपालव्यालचक्रवालविदलविहंगमेन्द्रस्य प्रचण्डदोर्दण्डखण्डिताभिनिवेशनानादेशनरेशभाललालितपादारविन्दस्य प्रबलपराक्रमाक्रान्तढिल्लीमण्डलगूर्जरत्रासुरत्राणदत्तातपत्रप्रथितहिन्दुसुरत्राणबिरुदस्य सुवर्णसत्रागारस्य षड्दर्शनधर्मार्थधारस्य चतुरङ्गवाहिनीवाहिनी पारावारस्य कीर्तिद्धर्मप्रजापालनसत्त्वादिगुणक्रियमाणश्रीरामयुधिष्ठिरादिनरेश्वरानुकारस्य राणश्रीकुम्भकर्णार्णसर्वोर्वीपतिसार्वभौमस्य 41 विजयमानराज्ये तस्य प्रसादपात्रेण विनयविवेकधैर्यौदार्यशुभकर्मनिर्मलशीलाद्भुदगुणमणिमयाभरणभासुरगात्रेणा श्रीमदहम्मदसुरत्राणदत्तफुरमाणसाधुश्रीगुणराजसङ्घपतिसाहचर्यकृताश्चर्य-कारिदेवालयाडम्बरपुरः सरश्रीशुंत्रजयादितीर्थयात्रेण अजाहरिपिण्डरवाटकसालेरादिबहुस्थाननवीनजैनविहारजीर्णोद्धारपदस्थापनाविषमसमयसत्रागारनानाप्रकारपरोपकारश्रीसङ्घसत्काराद्यगण्यपुरण्यमहार्घक्रयाणक पूर्यमाणभवर्णावतावरणक्ष-मननुष्यजन्मयानपात्रेण प्राग्वाटवंशावतंससं० सांगरसुत सं०कुरपाल भा० कामलदेपुत्रपरमार्हत सं०धरणाकेन ज्येष्ठभ्रातृ सं० रत्न भा० रत्नादेपुत्रसं०लाषाराजासोनासालिगस्वभा० सं० धारलंदेपुत्रजाङ्गाजाव-डादिप्रवर्द्धमानसन्तानयुतेन राणपुरनगरे राणाश्रीकुम्भकर्णार्णनरेन्द्रेण स्वनाम्ना निवेशिततदीयसुप्रसादादेशतस्त्रैलोक्यदीपकाभिधानः श्रीचतुर्मुखयुगादीश्वरविहारः कारितः प्रतिष्ठितः श्री बृहत्तपागच्छे श्रीजगच्चन्द्रसूरिश्रीदेवेन्द्रसूरीसन्ताने श्रीमत्श्रीदेवसुन्दरसूरिपट्टप्रभाकरपरमगुरुसुविहितपुरन्दरगच्छाधिराजश्रीसोमसुन्दर-सूरिभिः ॥कृतमिदं च सूत्रधारदेपाकस्य अयं च श्रीचतुर्मुखविहार आचन्द्रार्क नन्दतात्॥
शुभं भवतु॥

IV

The date of composition of Sangitaraja as given at the end of a manuscript copy of it in the Bikaner State Library is Wednesday the 13th day of the dark half of *Kartika*, Sambat 1509, Shaka year 1374 (11th October, A.D. 1456)

श्रीमद्विक्रमकालतः परिगते नंदाभ्रतक्षितौ
वर्षेक्षान्घनलेन्दुशाकसमये संवत्सरे च ध्रुवे।
ऊर्जे मासि तिथौ हरे र(क)विदिनेहस्तर्क्षयोगे तथा
योगे चाभिजिति स्फुटोयमभवतसंगीतरजाभिधः॥

V

The Kumbhalgarh Inscription, dated *Magsar Bad 5*, V.S. 1517 (A.D. 1460) engraved on stone tablets originally fixed in the Mamadeva (Kumbhaswāmi) Temple, and now kept in the Museum at Udaipur.

(Third slab)

॥अथ राजवर्णनं॥
अतः श्रीराजवंशोत्र प्रव्यक्तः (प्रोच्यते) धुना।
चिरंतनप्रशस्तीनामनेकानामतः क्षणात् ॥138॥

(Fourth slab)

माद्यन्माद्यन्महेभप्रखरकरहतिक्षिप्तराजन्ययूथो
यं खानः पत्तनेशो दफर इति समासाद्य कुण्ठीबभूव।

सोयं मल्लो रणदि: शककुलवनितादत्त वैधव्यदीक्ष:
कारगारे यदीये नृपतिशतयुते संस्तरं नापि लेभे ॥196॥
यात्रोच्चङ्कतुरंगचंचलखुराघातोच्छितै रेणुभि:
सेहे यस्य न लुप्तरश्मिपटलव्याजात्प्रतापं रवि:।
तच्चित्रं किमु सादलादिकनृपा यत्प्राकृतास्त्रसु—
स्त्यक्त्वास्वानि पुराणि कस्तुबलिनां सूक्ष्मो गुर्वा पुर:॥199॥
शस्त्राशस्त्रिहताजिलंपटभटव्रातोच्छलच्छोणित—
च्छन्नप्रोद्गातपांशुपुंजविसरत्प्रादुर्भवत्कर्दमम्।
त्रस्त: सामिहतो रणे शकपतिर्यस्मात्तथामालव—
क्ष्मापोऽद्यापि यथा भयेन चकित: स्वप्नेऽपि तं पश्यति ॥200॥

अमीसाहिरग्रहि येनाहिनेव
स्फुरद्भेक एकांगवीरव्रतेन।
जगत्त्राणकृद्यस्यपाणौ कृपाण:
प्रसिद्धोऽभवद्भूपति: खेतराण:॥202॥

कीनाशपाशान् सकलानपास्यत् यस्त्रिस्थलीमोचनत: शकेभ्य:।
तुलादिदानातिभरो व्यतारील्लक्ष्याख्यभूपो निहतप्रतीप: ॥207॥
मेदानाराद्वलसादुल्लसत्तद्भेदरीधीरध्वानविध्वस्तधैर्यान्।
कारं कारं यो ग्रही दुग्रतेजा दग्धारातिर्वर्द्धनाख्यं गिरीन्द्रम् ॥212॥

....

अथ महाराजाधिराजरायरायराणेराय—
महाराणाश्रीकुम्भकर्णवर्णनम् ॥232॥

माभूक्षुभ्यदनुच्छदुग्धजलधिस्वच्छोच्छलद्धीचिरु—
त्रक्तसत्कृतपूर्वपुरुषयशस्तत्संकुचद्धत्तिमत्।
इत्थं चारु विचार्यकुम्भनृपतिस्तानेकलिंगे व्यधात्
रम्यान् मणडपहेमदणडकलशांस्त्रैलोक्यशोभातिगान् ॥241॥

या नारदीयनगरावनिनायकस्य
नार्या निरंतरमचीकरदत्रदास्यम्।
तां कुम्भकर्णनृपतेरिहकः सहेत
बाणवलीमसमसंगरसंचरिष्णोः ॥246॥
योगिनीपुरमजेयमप्यसौ योगिनीचरणकिंकरो नृपः।
कुन्तलाकालतवैरिसुन्दरीविभ्रमे रमितविक्रमोऽगृहीत् ॥247॥
अरिन्दमः स्वांघ्रिसरोजलग्नं विशोध्य शोध्याधिपतिप्रतीपम्।
अरुंतुदं कणटकमिद्धतेजा भंक्त्वा क्षिपद्भूमिलतेऽसिसूच्या ॥248॥
येन वैरिकुलं हत्वा मंडोवरपुरग्रहे।
अनायि शांतिं रोषाग्निर्नारीनयनांबुभिः ॥249॥
विगृह्य हम्मीरपुरं शरोत्करैर्निगृह्य तस्मिन् रणवीरविक्रमम्।
नरसग्रहीदंबुजमंजुलोचना महीमहेन्द्रो नरपालकन्यकाः ॥250॥
नानादिग्भयो राजकन्याः समेत्य क्षोणीपालं कुम्भकर्णं श्रयंते।
सत्यं रत्नं जायते सागरादौ युक्तं विष्णोर्वक्ष एवास्य धाम ॥251॥
स धन्यो धान्यनगरमामूलादुदमूलयत्।
पुरारिविक्रमो यागपुरं पुरमिवाजयत् ॥253॥
ज्वालावलीवलयितां हतनोधवालीं
मन्त्रीरवीरमुदवीवहदेष नीरं।
यो वर्द्धमानगिरिमाशु विजित्य तस्मिन्
मेवानमंदमदबद्धविधीनधाक्षीत् ॥254॥
जनकाचलमुच्चशेखरं बलवन्मालवनाथमस्तके।
प्रवरं गिरिदुर्गमुद्धतश्चरणं वामिव न्यधादयम् ॥256॥
महोच्चाजनकाचले निखिलमालवक्ष्मापते—
गलेपदमिवन्यधादमितविक्रमो भूपतिः।
सरांसि जयवर्द्धने कृतपुरेऽपि यो वर्द्धने

APPENDIX 157

महामहिमशेखरे विपुलवप्रमुग्रद्युतिः ॥२५७॥
जनकाचलमग्रहीदलं महतीं चंपवतीमतीतपत्
गिरिसुन्दरखोलखंडनावनिवज्रायुध एष भूपतिः ॥२५८॥
प्रत्यर्थिपार्थिवपराजयजन्महेतुर्वृंदावतीपुरमदीदहदेष वीरः।
तद्गर्गराटगिरिदुर्गमपि क्षणेन संक्षोभमापयद पार पराक्रमेणा ॥२५९॥
मल्लारणयपुरं वरेणयमनलज्वालावीलढं वयधा—
द्वीरः सिंहपुरीमबीभरदसिप्रध्वस्तवरिरजैः।
यलं रत्नपुरप्रभंजनविधावाधायधीमानतो
नायं नायमनेकराजनिकरान् कारग्रहेवीवसत् ॥२६०॥
पदातीनां पादलक्षं सपादलक्षमावृतम्।
कृत्वा मल्लारणावीरो रणास्तंभं तथाजयत् ॥२६१॥
आर्मदाद्रिदलनेन दारुणाः कोटडाकलहकेलिकेसरी।
कुम्भकरार्णनृपतिर्बबावदो धूलनोद्धतभुजो विराजते ॥२६२॥
नम्रानेकनृपालमौलिनिकरप्रात्युप्तहीरांकुर—
श्रेणीरश्मिमिलन्नरवद्द्युतिभरः शत्रून् रणप्रांगणो।
दीर्घांदोलितबाहुदंडविलसत्कोदंडदंडोल्लस—
द्बाणसतान्विचरय्य मणडलकरं दुर्गं क्षणोनाजयत् ॥२६३॥
जित्वा देशंमनेकदुर्गविषमं हाडावटीं हेलया
तन्नाथान् करदान्विधाय च जयस्तंभानुदस्तंभयत्।
दुर्गं गोपुरमत्रषटपुरमपि प्रौढां च वृंदावतीं
श्रीमन्मंडल दुर्गमुच्चविलस्च्छालां विशालां पुरीम् ॥२६४॥
उत्खातमूलं सलिलैः प्रभंजन इव द्रुमं।
विशालनगरं राजा समूलमुदमूलयत् ॥२६५॥
तन्नागरीनयननीरतरंगिणीना—
मंगीकृतं किमु समुत्तरणां तुरगैः।

श्रीकुम्भकरार्णानृपतिः प्रवितीरार्णाभिपै—
रालोडयद्गिरिपुरं यदमीभिरुग्रः ॥266॥
यदीयगज्जद्गजतूर्यघोषसिंहस्वनाकर्णाननष्टशौर्यः ।
विहाय दुर्गं सहसा पलायां चकार गोपालश्रृगालबालः ॥267॥
त्यक्त्वा दीनादीनाधिनाथा दीना बद्धा येन सारंगपुर्याम् ।
योषाःप्रौढाः पारसीकाधिपानां ताः संख्यातुं नैव शक्रोति कोपि ॥268॥
गर्जन् म्लेच्छतिमिंगिलाकुलतरं रंगत्तुरंगोर्मिमन्
मातंगोद्धतनक्रचक्रममितं प्राकारवेलाचलं ।
एतद्ग्धपुराग्निवाडवमसौ यन्मालवांभोनिधिं
क्षोणीशः पिबति स्म खङ्गचुलकैस्तसमादगस्त्यः स्फुटं ॥270॥

VI

The Chitor *Kirtisthambha* (Tower of Victory)
Inscription, dated *Magsar Bad 5*, V.S. 1517 (A.D. 1460).

(Part I)

येनानर्गलमल्लदीर्णहृदया श्रीचित्रकूटांतिके
तत्तत्सैनिकघोरवीरनिनदप्रध्वस्तधैर्योदया ।
मन्ये यावनवाहिनी निजपरित्राणास्य हेतोरलं
भूनिःक्षेपमिषेण भीपरवशा पातालमूलं ययौ ॥22॥
संग्रामाजिरसीम्निशौर्यविलसद्दोर्दंडहेलोल्लस—
च्चाप प्रोद्गतबाणवृष्टिशमितारातिप्रतापानलः ।
वीरश्रीरणमल्लमूर्जितशकक्ष्मापालगर्वांतकं
स्फूर्जद्गूर्जरमंडलेश्वरमसौ कारागृहे वीवसत् ॥23॥

अमोचयद्घवनकराद्गयामयं तुलाव्यधादमितपराक्रमोमिताः ।
अपूज्यत्कनकभरैर्महीसुरानकारयत्सुरनिलयान्महोन्नतान् ॥31॥
मेदानाराद्ध्वसादुध्वसत्तद्भेदरीधीरध्वानविध्वस्त धैर्यान् ।
कारं कारं योगृहीदुग्रतेजा दग्धारातिर्वर्द्धनाख्यं गिरींद्रं ॥36॥

(Part II)

प्रतीपभूपालशिरत्सुवामं पदं निधाय क्षितिवल्लभेन ।
आनीयमांडव्यपुराद्धनूमान् संस्थापितः कुम्भलमेरुदुर्गं ॥3॥
सुग्रीवनीलांगदभूषितोसौ श्रीकुम्भकरार्णाश्चरितेन रामः ।
इतीव मांडव्यपुरात्समेत्य हनूमता................... ॥4॥
सपादलक्षं करदं विधाय शांकंभरीं चारुरमां गृहीत्वा ।
अपाठयत्संततमत्र वेदपारायणां वेदपरायणोऽसौ ॥5॥
कुम्भकर्णानृपतिः करप्रदं डिंहुआणलवणाकरं व्यधात् ।
यन्त्राणानगरीरणांगणो ससृहं विवृणुते जयश्रियः ॥6॥
विजित्य सकलं राज्यमादाय सकलां श्रियं ।
मुदाफरमदच्छेदमकार्षात्कुम्भभूपतिः ॥7॥
महामुनिश्रेष्ठवशिष्ठयोगपवित्रचित्रानलकुणडशोधि ।
असौ महौजाः प्रवरं वसंतपुरं व्यधत्ताभिनवो वसंतः ॥8॥
सप्तसागरविजित्वरानसौ सप्तपल्वलरानकारयत् ।
श्रीवसंतपुरनाम्नि चक्रिणाः प्रीतये वसुमतीपुरंदरः ॥9॥
अमराधिपप्रतिमवैभवो नृपो गिरिदुर्गराजमधिकुम्भमणडपं ।
स्फुरदेकलिङ्गनिलयाच्चपूर्वतो निरमापयत्सकलभूतलाद्भुतं ॥10॥
पोद्धाविधाटीपटुभिस्तरंगैर्विगाह्य गोकर्णागिरि नरेंद्रः ।
समग्रहीदर्बुदशैलराजं व्याधूययुद्धोद्धरधीरधुर्यान् ॥11॥

नीलाभ्रलिहमर्बुदाचलमसौ प्रौढप्रतापांशुमा—
नारोह्याखिलसनिकानसिबले नाजावजेयोजयत्।
निर्मायचलदुर्गमस्य शिखरे तत्राकरोदालयं
कुम्भस्वामिन उच्चशेखरशिखं प्रीत्य रमाचक्रिणोः ॥12॥
अर्बुदाचलशिरोवर्तंसिकां सर्वपार्थिवशिरोमणिर्मडान्।
निर्जितारिकरतुष्टबंधनात्तीर्थसंहतिमसावमोचयत् ॥14॥
चतुरश्चतुरो जलाशयान् चतुरो वारिनिधीनिवापरान्।
स किलार्बुदशेखरे नृपः कमलाकामुककेलये व्यधात् ॥15॥
स्फूर्जद्गुर्जरदेशदाहनविधावुद्दामधूमावलीं
यामुद्धेलवतीं व्यचीकरदिलां वेलाविधं सर्वतः।
यस्तस्यामुदजम्भतः प्रियतमाधमिललमंजुद्युति—
र्जानीमो गगनस्थलं मलिनिमा सोयं समालिंगति ॥16॥
श्रीकुम्भो मालवांभोधिनाथमंथलुमहीधरः।
अखर्वमकरद्गव महंमदमहीपतेः ॥17॥
शेषांगद्युतिगर्वरुन्नर पतेय स्येंदुधामोज्ज्वला
कीर्तिः शेषसरस्वतीविजयिनी यस्यामला भारती।
शेषस्यातिधरः क्षमाभरभृतो यस्योरुशैयोंभुजः
शेषं नागपुरं निपात्य च कथाशेष व्यधाद्भूपतिः ॥18॥
शकाधिपानां व्रजतामधस्ताद्दर्शयन्नागपुरस्य मार्गं।
प्रज्चाल्य पेरोजमशीतिमुच्चां निपात्य तन्नागपुरं प्रवीरः ॥19॥
निपात्य दुर्गं परिखां प्रपूर्य गजान् गृहीत्वा यवनीश्च बध्वा।
अदंडयद्यो यवनानतान् विडंबयन् गुर्जरभूमिभतुः ॥20॥
लक्षाणि च द्वादश गोमवल्लीरमोचयद् दुर्यवनानलेभ्यः।
तं गोचरं नागपुरं विधाय चिराय यो ब्राह्मणासादकाषीत् ॥21॥
मूलं नागपुरं महच्छकतरोरुन्मूल्य नूनं मही—

नाथोयं पुनरच्छिदतस्मदहत्पश्चान्मशीत्यासह।
तस्मात्प्लानिमवाप्य दूदमपतत् शाखाश्चपत्रारायहो
सत्यं याति न को विनाशमधिकं मूलस्य नाशे सति ॥22॥
अग्रहीद्रमितरत्नसंचयं कोशलः समसखानभूपतेः।
जांगलस्थलमगाहाहवे कुम्भकर्णाधरणीपुरंदरः ॥23॥
...... समुद्धससितवान् कासिलीं सहसाजयत्।
यस्य दुन्दुभिनिध्वानो धुंखराद्रि जयोद्भवः ॥24॥
आकर्णकुण्डलितचापविनिर्गतोरु—
बाणावलीविददलितारिबलो नृपालः।
खंडेलखंडनविधिं व्यतनोदतुच्छ—
सैन्योच्छलद्बहलरेणुविलुप्तभानुः ॥25॥
असौ शिरोमंडनचंद्रतारां विचित्रकूटं किल चित्रकूट।
स्वरा.........मकरोन्महींद्रो महामहाभानुरिवोदयाद्रिं ॥26॥
सरांसि यत्रातितरान्महंति वहंति नीलारुणासारसाली।
विभांति तीरागततमानिनीनां मुखारविन्दप्रतिमाभिवात्र ॥27॥
कलाशाचलसुदरं हिमिगिरिप्रख्यं च सर्वकर्ष
नानाहेमघटावतंसकिरणमैरोहसंतं श्रियं।
सर्ववींतिलकोपमं मुकुटवच्छीचित्रकूटाचले
कुंभस्वामिन आलयं व्यरचयच्छीकुंभकर्णो नृपः ॥28॥
कैलाशस्य प्रतिनिधिरिदं शंकरस्यादहास
ज्योत्स्नाराशिः किमु हिमवतः कर्णिका भूधरस्य।
इत्थं। नानाविष्यविषयं चित्रकूटस्य शृंगे
रम्यं हर्म्य व्यरचयदिलाधीश्वरश्चक्रपाणेः ॥29॥
तदांतिके देवगृहान्महोच्चानलंकृतान् हेमघटावतंसैः।
अकारयच्चादिवराहगेहमनेकधाश्रीरमणास्य मूर्तिः ॥31॥

रामकुण्डममराधिपचापप्राज्यदीधितिमनोहरगेहं।
दीर्घिकाश्च जलयंत्रदर्शनव्यग्रनागरिकदत्तकौतुकाः ॥32॥
कीर्तिस्तंभमकारयत्सरणधीरभ्रंलिहाग्रं समा—
धीशा सर्वसुपर्वराजहरिति क्रीडानिवासं श्रियः।
यत्रागत्यसुरांगनाः सकलभूसाम्राज्यलीलानिधे—
रस्येंद्रस्य नितंबिनीजनकृतान् पश्यंति लीलारसान् ॥33॥
भानुः स्वं रथमेकचक्रमकरोन्मेरोसतटे पर्यटन्
नवासौ रथचक्रयुग्मसरणिं कर्तुं समर्थोभवत्।
उच्चैर्मेरुगिरेर्नवोदिनकरः श्रीचित्रकूटाचले
भव्यां सद्रथपद्धतिं जनसुखायाचूलमूलं व्यधात् ॥34॥
रामः सरामो विरथो महोच्चे पद्भ्यामगच्छत्किल चित्रकूटे।
इतीव कुंभेन महीधरेणा किमत्र रामाः सरथानियुक्ताः ॥35॥
शाखामृगार्थं किल सेतु................. रघुनन्दनोपि।
इतीव दुर्गे खलु रामरथ्यां स सेतुबंधामकरोन्महीन्द्रः ॥36॥
दृष्ट्वकं किल चित्रकूटमचलं सन्मेदिनीलोचनं
धात्रा निर्मितमत्रविस्मृतिमपि ज्ञात्वा विधातुर्नृपः।
मन्येत्रापि कनीनिकामिवसरी नेत्रोदस्व्यापिनीं
निर्मायापरगादिनन्दन इव स्रष्टा नवीनोभवत् ॥37॥
किमेतत्कैलाशः सिततरशिलाशेखरशिरा
हिमाद्रेर्वा शृंगं नृपहितभवानीप्रणिहितं।
यदालोक्याल्हादं भजति नितरां कौतुकिजनो
हनूमात्रामांकं व्यरचयदसौ गोपुरमिह ॥38॥
भैरवांकविशिखामनोरमा भाति भूपमुकुटेन कारिता।
पार्वणोंदुविमलोपल(भि)स्तिर्या सुरेन्द्रपुरगोपुरोपमा ॥39॥
नृपाः संसेवध्वं चरणाकमलं कुम्भनृपते—

APPENDIX 163

र्मया सम्बन्धं चेदनुभवितुमिच्छास्ति भवतां।
इति प्रायः शिक्षानिपुरकमलााधिष्ठिततनु—
र्महालक्ष्मीरथ्या नृपपरिवृढेनात्र रचिता ॥40॥
चामुण्डायाः कापितस्याः प्रतोली
भव्या भाति क्षमाभुजा निर्मितोच्चा
....
श्रेणीरश्मिसीपिताशामुखश्रीः ॥41॥
श्रीमत्कुम्भक्षमाभुजाकारितोर्वी—
.... रम्यलीलागवाक्षा।
तारारथ्या शोभते यत्र तारा—
श्रेणी...... संमिलत्तोरणाश्रीः ॥42॥
राजप्रतोली मणिरश्मिरक्ता सदिंद्रनीलद्युतिनीलकांतिः।
सस्फाटिका शारदवारिदश्रीर्विभाति सेन्द्रायुधमंडनेव ॥125॥
डर्वीमंडनमुच्चगोपुरमसौ माणिक्यसत्तोरणां
जीमूतं सपुरंदरीयु..... मिलन्मीनध्वजाडंबरं।
उद्यत्सौधसुधावदातकिरणश्रेणीशशांकोज्जलं
दुर्गं कुम्भलमेरुमूर्द्धिशखरे विन्ध्याचलस्यासृजत् ॥126॥
प्राकारमत्यद्भुतश्रीरकारयत् सत्कपिशीर्षकाढ्यं।
अभ्रंलिहाग्राणि गृहाणि(देवा)लयाननन्तानिमिताः प्रपाश्च ॥127॥
भूपालसौधावलिशीतरश्मिरश्मिप्रतानौरिव संपतद्भिः।
यो भाति सन्नीरकरैः समंताद्गंगाप्रवाहैरिव हैमनोद्धिः ॥128॥
सरस्फुरत्तामरसान्तरालविशत्सदिंदीवरशोभि यत्र।
मरालवाचालविशालवीचिछटोच्छलच्चंचल चक्रवाकं ॥129॥
तत्र तोरणलसन्मणिकुम्भस्वामिमंदिरमकारयन्महत्।
भूपतिः सकलभूतलाद्भुतं चक्रपाणिचरणार्च्चनापरः ॥130॥

संनिधेस्य कुम्भनृपतिःसरोद्धुतं निरमापयत् शशिकलोज्जवलोदकं।
नरकिंनरासुरसुरांगनाजनो जलकेलयं श्रयति यत्समंततः ॥१३१॥
कनकवरणः प्रौढो नीलोत्पलद्युतिरंजित—
स्तरणिकिरणप्रौढतेजःप्रभारुणिताम्बरः।
जलदपटीलदीर्घोत्तुंगांचितो यदधित्यका
सुरपतिधनुर्लेखालक्ष्मीं बिभर्ति समंततः ॥१३२॥
आशापेक्षकृतोरुगोपुरमुखः सद्योगपट्टोपमः
प्रोदंचद्धरणः कमंडलुगलद्गंगः सरोवारिभिः।
रम्यस्फाटिकहर्म्यरश्मिपटलीकूर्चो विरंचिश्चिरं
शंके दुर्ग(मिषा)दमुत्र सकलां स्वीयां कृतिं पश्यति ॥१३३॥
मन्येस्फादिकहर्म्यरश्मिपटलैर्दीर्घोरुकूर्चायितं
वप्रेणापि सुमेरुसुंदररुचा यद्योगपट्टायितं
आशापेक्षकृतोच्चगोपुरवरैस्तस्योरुवक्रायितं
दुर्गेणापि विलोकितुं वसुमतीं ब्रह्मायितं चारुणा ॥१३४॥
भुजवलयचतुष्टयी.....खचितमणिनिचयाचतुर्भुजस्य।
चतस्रष्षु विशिखाचतुष्टयीयं स्फुरति(हरित्सु)च यत्र दुगवर्ये ॥१३५॥
चतुरर्णवमेखलैक दुर्गे चतुरंभोधिगतोरुरत्नराशिः।
प्रतिदिग्महतीर्व्यधत्त रथ्याः नृपतिर्ग्राहयितुं निजप्रतापैः ॥१३६॥
द्रष्टुं नालं समंतात्सकलनिजकृतिं द्वीपपायोधिवेला
विछिन्नां भूतधात्रीं सुरगृहभुजगागारलीलामितीव।
कुंभक्षोणींद्ररूपावतरणमधुनाश्रित्यमन्ये विधाता
सर्वामृद्धिदिक्षुः प्रमुदितहृदयः कुंभमेरुं व्यधत्त ॥१३७॥
जंबूद्वीपालं कृती कुंभमेरौ मेरौ स्तिष्ठनूकणिकाकारचारौ।
श्रीमत्कुंभक्षमापतिः पद्मनेत्रो मन्येधत्ते नवयपद्मासनत्वं ॥१३८॥
कणिकाकृतिधरसयसुमेरो......कुंभमाश्रितास्त्रयः।

APPENDIX 165

श्वेतनीलगिरिश‍ृंगिपर्वता भांति सेवितुमुपागता नृपं ॥139॥
विभ्राजी विपुलश्चात्र भ्राजते पश्चिमाश्रितः।
अर्बुदाद्रिनिरीक्षार्थमागताविव बांधवौ ॥140॥
हिमवान् हेमकूटश्च निषधोगंधमादनः।
यस्य दक्षिणदिग्भागं श्रयतीव महान्नताः ॥141॥
पूर्वतोवसति यस्य मंदरो मंदरा....सुन्दरः।
इंदिराचरणपंकजामलन्यासपूतशिखरो महीधरः ॥142॥
वृंदावनं चैत्ररथं च नंदनं मनोज्ञभृगं ध्वनिगंधमादनं।
नृपाललीलाकृतवाटिकामिषाढसंत्यमून्यत्र समेत्य भूधरे ॥143॥
अनल्पनेत्र....वैजयंतो महिममहेन्द्रः खलु कुंभकर्णः।
समाश्रितः कुंभलमेरुदुर्गं सुराधिराजं खलु कुंभकर्णः।
अप्यंकमीनध्वजमप्सनेकमीनध्वजं भाति नरेन्द्रदुर्गं।
अनेकचंद्रोपमपि स्फुटैकचंद्रप्रभेद्वासितसौधभागं ॥145॥
आनयद्द्विरदवक्रमादराद्व्हतप्रतिनृपालदुर्गतः।
दुर्गवर्यशिखरे निजे तथा स्थापयत्कृतमहोत्सवो नृपः ॥146॥
समकरोदचलेश्वरसन्निधावचलदुर्गमिसौ जगतीपतिः।
यवनवारवधादिव तोषितो मुकुटमर्बुदभूमिभृतो व्यधात् ॥147॥
योयं राजगुरुश्चदानगुरुरि.....प्रसिद्धश्च यो
योसौ शैलगुरुर्गुरुश्चपरमः प्रोद्दामभूमिभुजां।
यो......धिक वीरवंदितपदः प्राच्यप्रतीच्योत्तर—
प्रोद्यद्दक्षिणभूपमंडनमणिः कुंभो............... ॥148॥
नरेश्वरो धृष्टतमोतिस्पृतमहीभृदुन्मूलनमूलहेतुः।
विराजते दुर्बलभूमिपालसंस्थापनी.........तया नरेन्द्रः ॥149॥
असमसमरभूमीदारुणः कुंभकर्णः
करकलितकृपाणेर्वैरिवृंदं निहत्य।

चलितरुधिरपूरोत्तालकल्लोलिनीभिः
शमयति पितृवैरोद्भूतरोषानलौघं ॥150॥
आजावाजौ निहतविमतानीकिनीशोणितोघे
वारं वारं समरतरलां क्षालयित्वा कृपाणीं ।
दायं दायं विविधवसुधां वृत्तयेऽसौ द्विजेभ्यो
मन्ये नव्यः प्रभवतितरां भार्गवः कुंभदंभात् ॥151॥

आकुंभकर्णभुजविक्रमभीमसेन—
हिन्दूकराजगाजनायक मुंच मुचं ।
इच्छं रणेषु व्यलपन् परवीरधुर्या
यस्योरुबाणनिकराहति भीतिचिताः ॥152॥

सिंहासनासनासितातपवारणोरु-
माणिक्यमंडनचलच्चमराधिकोऽभूत् ।
आलोक्य मत्सरितमानसभूमिपाला-
नुव्यार्मिशिक्षयदयं विनयं नरेन्द्रः ॥153॥

अमूमुचच्चतुर्वेदविचारचतुराननः ।
गयां यवनकरातो..... स्तापसीमिव ॥155॥

पात्रसादकृतमादराद्द्विप्रसादकृतभूयसीभुवः ।
कृष्णसादकृतमानसं नृपः शास्त्रसादकृतहृष्टिगौरव । ॥156॥

आलोडयाखिलभारतीविलसितं संगीतराजं व्यधात्
औद्धत्यावधिरंजसा समतनोत्सूडप्रबन्धाधिमुं ।
नानालंकृतिसंस्कृतां व्यरचययच्चंडीशतव्याकृतिं
वागीशो जगतीतलं कलयति श्रीकुंभदभाक्तिल ॥157॥

येनाकारि मुरारि संगतिरसप्रस्यंदिनी नन्दिनी
वृत्तिव्याकृति चातुरीभिरतुला श्रीगीतगोविंदके ।
श्रीकर्णाटकमेदपाटसुमहाराष्ट्रादिके योदय—

द्राणीगुंफमयं चतुष्टयमयं सत्राटकानां व्यधात् ॥158॥
श्रीकुंभकर्णरचितामवलोक्य वाचं
माधुर्यधुर्यमपि गेयममुष्य मत्वा।
......न्महीपतिरनंतगुणोत्सुदारां
...........गिरमाद्रियते न कश्चित् ॥159॥
सकलकविनृपाली मौलिमणिक्यरोचि—
र्मधुररणितवीणावाद्यवे शद्यबिंदुः।
मधुकरकुललीलाहारि...... रसाली
जयति जयति कुंभो भूरिशौर्याशुमाली ॥160॥
तावत्कल्पतरुर्विभिर्ति विपुलस्तावच्च चिंतामणि—
सतावत्कामगवी च दानजनिभूसतावत्सुवर्णाचलः।
नोंयाव...... निमार्गणगणः श्रीकुंभकर्णों..... ते ॥161॥
चित्रं यत् कटकोत्थरेणुनिकरः.........मुखान्यश्नुते
मालिन्यं वरवैरिवीरवनितावक्त्रांबुजे जायते।
खङ्गे यस्य मदांधसिंधुरशिरः सिंदूरमेवाच्छिन—
त्सीमन्तादरियोषितामुद...... त्सिंदूरपूरश्रयत् ॥162॥
यस्यानर्गल दुर्गवर्गदलनव्यासक्तदोर्वल्लदरी
लीलोत्सारितवैरिवारणघटाघंटारवैवणिता।
कीर्तिः संप्रति संप्रतीपतरुणी कर्णावर्तंसायते
वैधव्येऽपि विडंबना हि विवशाः कां कां सहंते न तो ॥164॥
धीरोद्धतं समिति संसदि धीरशांत
मित्रेषु भूपतिष भूपमुदारधीरं।
कांतासु धीरललितं कलयंति संतो
ये नायकावलिगुण(ब्रज)जन्मभूमिं ॥165॥
नायिकानिचयलोचनोल्लसद्ववसंकरविनोदमंदिरं।

कुंभकर्णनृपतिर्महीतले मीनकेतनतुलामविंदत ॥166॥
नाटकप्रकरणांकवाथिकानाटिकासमवकारभणके।
प्रोल्लसत्प्रहसनादिरूपके नव्य एषभरतो महीपतिः ॥167॥
भारतीयरसभाववृष्टयः प्रेमचातकपयोदवृष्टयः।
नंदिकेश्वरमतानुवर्त्तनाराधितत्रिनयनं श्रयति यं ॥168॥
विक्रमद्रुमकुरंगकेतनोष्णेषयद्वयजय..... बृहन्नटः।
संतताधिगतधर्मशासन नावृकोदर इयं विचित्रता ॥170॥
श्रीभारतीरससमुद्भववकैरबोध—
दुद्यान...... .... कतमः समः स्यात्।
श्रीकुंभकर्णजगतीपतिना नवीन—
निर्माणचारुमतिना विधिनेव साक्षात् ॥171॥
स्फूर्ज्जद्गुर्जरमालवेश्वर सुरत्राणारुसन्याणव—
व्यस्ताव्यस्तसम स्तवारणवनप्राग्भारकुंभोद्भवः।
...... पार्थिवरणप्रारंभदीक्षागुरु—
र्णयः कुंभमहीपतिसुमतीविश्वेश्वरो राजते ॥172॥
अमंदमदसंभ्रमभ्रमितभृंगमालामिल—
त्कपोलतलवेल्लितः श्रवणातालवृंतानिलैः।
रणापहृतकुंजैरमित गूर्जराधीश्वरा—
.... भुजश्रमाः समिति कुंभभूमीभुजा ॥173॥
मेदपाटाब्धिसंजातरोहिणीरमणो नृपः।
कस्य नो नयनानंदं तनुतेऽवनिमंडले ॥174॥
विमतभूधरकुंजरकेसरी यवनसैन्यतृणौघदवानलः।
अकलयत्कलिकालकदर्थना परवशं... मनो न मनागपि ॥175॥
प्रत्यर्थिपार्थिवतमोनिचयप्रचंड—
चंडद्युतिर्जयति यस्य भुजप्रतापः।

सामंतभपतिनितंबवतीविलास—
प्रोल्लासिसारसतुषारकरः शरोपि ॥१७६॥
समस्तजगतीललप्रबल वैरिकंठाटवी—
नवीनदहनोच्चयोधरणिमंडलाखंडलः ।
कुरंगनयनामनः कुमुदवृंदशीनद्युतिः
प्रतापजितभानुमान् जयति कुंभकर्णोद्भुवं ॥१७७॥
हयेशहस्तीशनरेशराजत्रयोल्लसत्तोडरमल्लमुख्यं ।
विजिल्य तानाजिषु कुंभकर्णमहीमहेन्द्रो विरुदं बिभर्त्ति ॥१७८॥
तौरुष्कव्रजवाहिनीपरिलसत्पाथोधिवेलावलि—
व्यालीनावनिमुद्धरंतमवदन्नाद्य वराहं बुधाः ।
यं शीतांशुकलावतंसकलितप्राज्यप्रसादप्रभं
माद्यन्मालवमोदिनीश्वरमदच्छैदैकदीक्षागुरुं ॥१७९॥
यः श्रीमोकलभूपतेः समुदितः सौभाग्यभूमावपि
यं प्रासूतलसत्प्रतापतरणिं सौभाग्यदेवीसुतं ।
येनासाद्यगुरोः कलाश्चसकला दत्ता द्विजेभ्यो भुवं
भुंक्ते कुंभनरेश्वरः कुचभरा..... मिव प्रेयसीं ॥१८०॥
वेणीव्याजवलद्भुजंगललनालावरायलीलालया
सौंदर्यामृतदीर्घिकापरिलसन्नालीकनेत्रद्वया ।
कुंभारंभकुचद्वयोपरिचलन्नामुक्तमुक्ता च या
यस्यानंगकुतूहलकपदवीकृीोल्लदेवीप्रिया ॥१८१॥
सहस्रवदनो यदा वदति वीतवेद्यांतरः
सहस्रकरपल्लवो लिखति वेदविश्रांतधीः ।
अथस्फुरति भारतीक्वचनदेशिकेसौ यदा
गणयगुणसंततिर्भवति कुंभकर्णस्तदा ॥१८२॥
यावच्चंद्रदिवाकरौ हिमगिरिर्यावच्चहेमाचलो

यावत्सागरभूषण वसुमती यावच्च सेतुर्महान्।
तावत्तिष्ठतु कुंभकर्णनृपतिः कीर्तिप्रशस्तिसतथा
नानाकारितकीर्तनानि सकला साम्राज्यलक्ष्मीरपि ॥183॥
वर्षे पंचदशे शते व्यपगते सप्ताधिकेकार्तिक
स्याधानंगतितौ नवीनविशिखां श्रीचित्रकूटे व्यधात्।
उद्यत्तोणचारुहीरनिकरस्फीतप्रभाभासुर—
प्रोदं चेत्कपिशीर्षकांकितशिरो रम्यां महीवल्लभः ॥184॥
श्रीविक्रमात् पंचदशधिकेस्मिन् वर्षेशते पंचदशे व्यतीते।
चत्रासितेनंगतितौ व्यधापि श्रीकुंभमेरुर्वसुधाधिपेन ॥185॥
पुणये पंचदशे शते व्यपगते पंचाधिके वत्सरे
माघे मासि वलक्षपक्षदशमी देवेज्यपुष्यागमे।
कीर्तिस्तंभमकायन्त्ररपतिः श्रीचित्रकूटाचले
नानानिर्मितनिर्जरावतरणमेंरोहंसंतं श्रियं ॥186॥
सत्प्राकारप्रकारं प्रचुरसुरगृहडंबरं मंजुगुंज—
द्भृंगश्रेणीवरेणयोयवनपरिसरं सर्वसंसारसारं।
नंदव्योमेषु शीतद्युतिमिति रुचिरे वत्सरे माघमासे
पूर्णयांपूर्णरूपं व्यरचयदचलं दुग्गमुर्वीमहेन्द्रः ॥187॥

VII

Ekling Mahātmya
(of the time of Maharana Kumbha)

हेलोन्मूलितमल्लवंशककुदं बंदीकरत्नबुंदं
दुर्गाद्रावित दुष्टतापमृगकं भंक्त्वा पुरं वायसम्।
तीडामंडलमग्रहीच्च सहसा जित्वा शकं दुर्जयं
जीवव्याद्धर्षशतं स भृत्यतुरगः श्रीकुंभकर्णो भुवि ॥157॥

समकरोदचलेश्वरसन्निधावचलदुर्गमसौ जगतीपतिः।
यवनवारवधादिव तोषितो मुकुटमर्बुदभूमिभृतो व्यधात् ॥164॥
वेदा यन्मौलिरत्नं स्मृतिविहितमतं सर्वदा कणठभूष।
मीमांसे कुण्डले द्वे हृदि भरतमुनिव्याहृतं हारवल्ली।
सार्वज्ञं विभ्रदुच्चैरगणितगुणभूर्भासते कुम्भभूपः ॥172॥
अष्टव्याकरणी विकास्युपनिषत्सष्टाष्टदंष्टोत्कटः
षट्तक्कीविकटोक्तियुक्तिविसरत्प्रसफारगुंजारवः।
सिद्धातोद्धतकानैकवसतिः साहित्यभूक्रीडनो
गर्जद्धादिगणन्निदार्य..........प्रज्ञास्फुल्केसर ॥173॥
येनाकारिमुरारिसङ्गतिरस प्रस्यन्दिनी नन्दिनी —
वृत्तिर्व्याकृतिचातुरीभिरतुला श्री गीतगोविन्दके।
श्रीकर्णटकमेदपाटसुमहाराष्ट्रादिते योदय —
द्वाणी गुम्फमयं चतुष्टयमयं सन्नाटकानां व्यधात् ॥174॥
यः श्रुत्वा भरतं चतुर्भिरखिलैर्भाष्यैश्च रत्नाकरं
सोपायं बहुशो विलोक्य निखिलान्त्राघागमान् वीक्ष्य च।
गौरीनन्दिमते मतंगशिवसंगीते से शार्दूलके
दृष्ट्वा दंतिल दुर्गशक्तिभणतीस्तान्नाटदोक्तीरिप ॥202॥

VIII

The Eklingji Temple Inscription dated *Chait Sud* 10, V.S 1545 (Thursday 12th March, A.D. 1489).

संग्रामोद्धरविद्विषोद्धिष(द्धत)शिश्वाः शामित्रमंत्रेज्चलै —
रभुक्ष्य क्षणलक्षितार्थचरितः प्रोद्धासिधाराजलैः।
यौमीसाहिमहाहिगर्वगरलं मूलादवादीदहत्
सक्षत्रक्षितिभृत् प्रभूतविभवः श्रीचित्रकूटेऽभवत् ॥29॥

प्राकारमैलमभिभृत् विधूय वीरान्—
आदाय कोशमखिलं खलु खेतासिंहः ।
कारांधकारमनयद्रणमल्लभूप-
मेतन्महीमकृततसुतसात्प्रसह्य ॥30॥
दंडाखंडितचंडमंडलकरप्राचीनमाचूर्णयत्
तन्मध्योद्यतधीरयोधनिधनं निर्माय निर्मायधीः ।
हाडामंडलमुंडखंडन धृतसफूर्ज्जत्कूबंधोद्धरं
कृत्वा संगरमात्मसाद्धसुमतीं श्रीखेतसिंहो व्यधात् ॥31॥
जोगादुगांधि(पं यः)समरभुवि पराभूय लक्षः क्षितींद्रः
कन्यारत्नान्यहार्षीत्सहगजतुरगैयौंवराज्यं प्रपन्नः ।
प्रत्यूहव्यूहमिहं प्रणिधिभिखधूयाखिलं राजवृत
निर्व्याजं जागरूको हरचरणरतः पैत्र्यराज्यं बुभोज ॥35॥
सत्पक्षः प्रतिपक्षलक्षबलभिञ्जिष्णुर्महासंगरे
दूतानंतस्युन्मिषन्मखरतिः श्रीमोकलो भूपतिः ।
आजि जाजपुरे प्रभूतपुरुषैरालभ्यदंमोलिभृन्न-
व्यो नाथधराधरोद्दुरशिरः सकंधानभांक्षीत्क्षणात् ॥43॥
कौ कुणितकर्णधरविभवः श्रीमोकलो भूधवः
प्रौढिं नावमुयेयुषो जलचरः पीरोजपृथ्वीभुजः ।
स्कंधावारमपारवारणमजद्धाजिब्रजव्याकुलं
व्यावलगत्तरवारिवारिणी रणकूपारगर्भेक्षिपत् ॥44॥

Bibliography

BOOKS (ENGLISH)

1. *Annals and Antiquities of Rajasthan*, by Col. James Tod, 2 Vols., London, A.D. 1829–32.
2. *Travels in Western India*, by Col. James Tod.
3. *Muhammadan Dynastics of India*, by Stanley Lane Pool, A.D. 1894.
4. *History of the Rise of the Muhammadan Power in India*, by J. Brigg (Ferishta's *History of India*).
5. *History of Gujrat*, by Sir E.C. Bayley, A.D. 1886.
6. *Indian Ephemeris*, by Diwan Bahadur L.D.S. Pillai.
7. *History of Mediæval Hindu India*, by C.V. Vaidya.
8. *History of Indian and Eastern Architecture*, by James Fergusson.
9. *Memoirs of Jahangir*, by Alexander Rogers, (Translation of *Tuzaki Jahangeri*.)
10. *History of India, as told by its own Historians*, by Sir E.C. Elliot, Vols. I–VIII.
11. *Outline of History*, by H.W. Wells.
12. *Archæological Survey Reports of India*, Vols. VI for A.D. 1872–

73, and XXIII for 1883–84; and the Annual Report for A.D. 1907-8.
13. *A Collection of Prakrit and Sanskrit Inscriptions*, published by the Bhavanagar Archæological Department under the auspices of the Maharaja of Bhavanagar, by Peter Peterson. Short title, "*The Bhavanagar Inscriptions.*"
14. *Gazetteer of Udaipur*, by Major K.D. Erskine.
15. *Proceedings of the First Indian Oriental Conference*, Poona, A.D. 1919.
16. *Progress Report of the Archaeological Survey of India*, Western Circle, for 1908–9.
17. *Report of a Second Tour in Search of Sanskrit Manuscripts in Rajputana and Central India*, by Prof. S.R. Bandarkar in 1905-6.
18. *Historical Fragments of the Mughal Empire, of the Morattoes &c.*, by Robert Orme, A.D. 1805.
19. *Early History of India*, by Dr. Vincent Smith.
20. *The Bombay Gazetteer Vol. I.*, by J.M. Campbell.
21. *Reports of the Rajputana Museum, Ajmer*, for 1917–1918, 1921, 1922, 1924 and 1926.
22. *Catalogue of Manuscripts Existing in the Central Provinces*, by F. Keilhorn.
23. *Catalogue Catalogorum*, by Aufrecht, Leipzig.
24. *Ajmer: Historical and Descriptive*, by the Author.
25. *Hammira of Ranthambhor*, by the Author. A monograph on Hammir, the renowened Chauhan King of Ranthambhor, one of the great heroes of Rajputana. An account of his conquests, and a full account of his war with Sultan Allauddin Khilji is given.

JOURNALS

26. *The Indian Antiquary*, Vol. 40.
27. *Epigraphia Indica*, Vol. II.

28. *Journal of the Bombay Branch of the Royal Asiatic Society*, G.B. & Ireland, Special No. LVIII by Captain E. Barnes, A.D. June 1902.
29. *The Krita, Gupta, Saka and other Eras* in the Modern Review for A.D. July, 1932.
30. *Journal of the Bengal Asiatic Society*, Volume 55.
31. *The Vedic Magazine of Aswin*, S. 1969. (A.D. 1912).
32. *The Udaipur Temple of Malwa* by K.P. Jaiswal in the Modern Review for A.D. June, 1932.

SANSKRIT

33. The *Eklinga Mahatmya*.
    A Sanskrit poem written during the time of Maharana Kumbha, who wrote a part of it. The Chapter headed *Rajvarnana Adhyaya*, contains verses from various old inscriptions giving the geneology of the Rulers of Mewar. (Unpublished).
34. *Rasik Priya*, (Nirnaya Sugar Press, Bombay.) It is a commentary by Maharana Kumbha on Jaideva's celebrated lyric poem, *Gita Govind*. It contains a short account of Maharana Kumbha and his predecessors.

HINDI

35. Barva Devidan's *Bahi*. (Unpublished).
    It is a record kept by the State geneologist of the geneologies of the kings of Mewar and contains various matters of historical importance.
36. "*Aitihasik Baton ka Sangrah*" by Kaviraj Bankey Das. (Unpublished).
    It is a miscellaneous record of historical events and interesting incidents of the lives of various historical personages, Hindus,

Muslims, Marhattas. Kaviraj Bankey Das was the Court poet of Maharaja Man Singh of Marwar, and lived in Jodhpur in the 19th century. It is a most valuable collection of miscellaneous historical information in the Marwari language.

37. *Mehta Nainsi's Khyat* (Chronicles).

    Mehta Nainsi was the Prime Minister of Maharaja Jaswant Singh I of Jodhpur. The book contains very valuable historical information about the various States of Rajputana and other parts of India, such as Bundelkhand, Rewa, Kathiawar, Cutch, etc. It was written in the old Marwari language between A.D. 1648 and 1664. A Hindi rendering of it is being published by the Nagri Pracharini Sabha, Benares.

38. *Vir Vinod*, by M.M. Kaviraja Shamal Das.

    It gives an exhaustive account of the history of Mewar, and brief histories of the other States of Rajputana, Kathiawar and other parts of India, and of the Sultans of Malwa, Gujrat, etc., and the Moghal Emperors of Delhi. It was written under the orders of Maharana Sajjan Singh of Mewar (A.D. 1874 to A.D. 1884). It was printed in two parts containing about 3,000 pages quarto. It is not published.

39. *Prachin Lekh Sangrah*, by Muni Jin Vijai.

    It is a collection of Jain inscriptions found in Rajputana, Gujarat and other places, and was printed at Bhavanagar in A.D. 1921.

40. Jodhpur *Khyat* or Marwar *Khyat* (Unpublished).

    It is a history of the Jodhpur State in the Marwari language compiled during the reign of Maharaja Man Singh (A.D. 1803–43).

41. *Udaipur ka Itihas*, (History of Udaipur) by Mahamahopadhyaya Pandit Gauri Shankar Ojha.

42. *Sirohi ka Itihas*, (History of Sirohi) by Mahamahopadhyaya Pandit Gauri Shankar Ojha.

43. *Maharana Yash Prakash*, by Thakur Bhur Singh of Malsisar (Jaipur).

It is a collection of old poems eulogising the deeds of the various Maharanas of Mewar, with Hindi translations.
44. *Devakulapataka*, by Vijayadharmsuri.
It is a collection of Jain inscriptions found in the various temples at Delwara in the Udaipur State.
45. *Nagri Pracharni Patrika*, New series, Benares.
A quarterly journal of historical and literary research, published by the Nagri Pracharini Sabha of Benares.

PERSIAN

46. The *Mirati Sikandari*.
A History of Gujarat by Sikandar-bin-Muhammad, written in A.D. 1611. (See *Bayley's History of Gujarat*.)
47. *Tarikhi Alfi* by Maulana Ahmad and others.
(See Elliot's *History of India*, Vol. V, p. 150.)
48. *Akbarnama* by Abul Fazal.
49. *Wakiati Mushtaqi* by Rizaqulla Mushtaki. See Elliot's *History of India*, Vol. IV, p. 532.

INSCRIPTIONS

1. The (Chitor) *Samiddeshwar* (Mokalji) *Temple Inscriptions of Magh Sud 3*, V.S. 1485 (A.D. 1429). It is published in the *Epigraphia Indica*, Vol. II, p. 410, and also in the Bhavanagar Inscriptions, p. 96.
It is a long inscription containing 80 Sanskrit verses. It records the erection (renovation) of the temple of Samiddeshwar, and mentions the names of the Guhil rulers of Mewar from Ari Singh to Mokal, and says that Maharana Lakha freed the holy place Gaya, from the distress brought upon it by the Muhammadans. His son Mokal defeated Feroz Khan of Nagor,

and built the temple of Vishnu and excavated a tank near it.

2. The Eklingji Temple Inscription of *Chait Sud* 10, S. 1545 (A.D. 1489). It is published in the Bhavanagar Inscriptions, p. 117. This also is a long inscription containing 100 Sanskrit verses. It records the various gifts of villages for the maintenance of the temple, and mentions the wars waged by Maharanas Mokal, Kumbha and Rāi Mal with the Muslim Kings of Delhi and Gujrat. The writer, Maheshwar, was Poet Leaurate of Mewar in Maharana Rāi Mal's time.

3. The Shringirishi Inscription of *Sawan Sud* 5, S. 1485 (A.D. 1428) (Unpublished). It was engraved on a slab built into a wall at Shringirishi about 6 miles from Udaipur. The slab broke into 6 pieces, 3 of which are missing. A summary of it is given in the Report of the Rajputana Museum, Ajmer, for A.D. 1924–25. It records that Rana Hammir took Chelakhyapur (Jilwara) from the Bhils. He killed Jaitreshwar (Jaitsi of Idar) and burnt the town of Prahladandpur (Palanpur in Gujarat). His son Kshetra Singh defeated Ami Shah (of Malwa) and took Mandalgarh from his enemies. Mokal defeated Feroz Khan (of Nagor) and got himself weighed against gold and silver 25 times, once in the *Adi Varah Temple* in Pushkar. It also mentions that Mokal erected a rampart round the temple of Eklingji, with 3 gates, and constructed a well at Shringirishi for the spiritual welfare of his wife, Gaurambika of the Baghel family.

(All the verses from the 3 Inscriptions described above—the Samiddheshwar Temple Inscription, the Eklingji Temple Inscription and the Shringirishi Inscriptions—to which references have been made in this book, are given in original in the Appendix.)

4. *Goganda Seetlamata Temple* Inscription of *Ashadh Bad* 13, V.S. 1423 (A.D. 1366). (Unpublished). It records the construction of a temple during the reign of Rana Kshetra Singh.

5. *An Inscription in the baodi* (tepped wall) *at Ghosundi*, near Chitor, of Baisakh Sud 3, V.S. 1561 (A.D. 1504). It is published in the *Journal of the Bengal Asiatic Society*, Vol. LVI, part I, p. 79. It records the construction of a *baodi* by Shringar Devi, daughter of King Jodha of Marwar and wife of Maharana Rāi Mal, son of Maharana Kumbhakarna.

6. *Jawar Inscription of the Temple of Ramaswami*, dated *Chaitra Sud* 7th, V.S. 1554 (A.D. 1497). (Unpublished). The Inscription is engraved on a stone slab built into a niche in a *Kund* (water reservoir) near the temple of Ramaswami. It is in 3 pieces and contains 40 verses. It states that the temple of Ramaswami and Ramakund were built by Ramabai, daughter of Maharana Kumbhakarna, and wife of Raja Mandik of Sorath, at Jawar. See Rajputana Museum Report for A.D. 1924–25.

7. *Kot Solankian Inscription* of *Ashadha Sud* 3, V.S. 1475 (A.D. 1419) published in the *Journal of the Bengal Asiatic Society*, Vol XII, p. 115. It records that during the reign of Rana Lakha, the *Mandap* of the Paraswanath Temple was repaired by Saha Kadua and members of his family.

8. *Jawar Shantinath Temple Inscription*, dated *Pos Sud* 6, V.S. 1478 (A.D. 1421) engraved on a lintel of the temple. It is published in *Prachin Jain Lekh Sangrah*, Vol. II, p. 22, by Muni Jin Vijaya. A summary of it is given in the Report of the Rajputana Museum for 1924–1925, p. 3. It records that the temple of Shantinath was erected by the descendants of Saha Nana of the Pragvat (Porvad) family.

9. *The Rāja Prashasti*, dated *Magh Sud* 15, S. 1732 (A.D. 1676). It is an epic poem in 24 cantos, engraved on 25 slabs, each slab containing a canto, and a preliminary slab containing laudatory verses. The slabs are fixed in the niches of the embankment of the Lake *Raj Samudra* constructed by Maharana Raj Singh (A.D. 1652–1680.) A short summary of it is published in the Report of the Rajputana Museum, Ajmer for A.D. 1917-18 pp. 2-3.

It describes the history of the family of the Maharanas, and says that the construction of the lake *Raj Samudra* was begun in A.D. 1665 and finished in A.D. 1676. It mentions that Bappa conquered Chitor from the Mori king Mān and adopted the title of Rawal. His descendant Rawal Karan son of Rahap, defeated Mokalsi of Mandor and adopted his title of Rana, and took up residence at Chitor. It describes the wars waged by Maharanas Kumbhā, Sāngā, and Pratap. It mentions a curious incident of a *Bhat* (bard). Maharana Pratap had given a turban to a *Bhat* who, when he went to Akbar's Darbar, took the turban off and held it in his hand when bowing. In explanation of this insult to the Emperor, he said that the turban was of the unconquered Pratap.

It describes how peace was concluded after the war between Emperor Jahangir and Maharana Amar Singh. The inscription mentions that prince Khurrum (later Shah Jahan) under orders from Jahangir, came to Rana Amar Singh to have a friendly talk, and that the prince then concluded a treaty of peace.

Maharana Raj Singh's conquests of Ajmer, Sambhar, Shahpura, Jahazpur, Ranthambhor, Bayana, Toda, Lalsote, Tonk, Malpura and other places are mentioned. The conquest of Sirohi and the Maharana's marriage with the daughter of the Raja of Kishengarh who had been previously betrothed to Emperor Aurangzeb are then described. Further on, a description of the lake, its construction, its measurements, and other things are given. A full account of the visits of the Maharaja of Jodhpur, Jaipur, Bikaner, Jaisalmer, Bundi, Rewa and others who came as guests at the consecration ceremony, which cost 7 lakh rupees, is then given. Aurangzeb's invasion of Mewar is described. The inscription describes the sack of Badnagar, Ahmadnagar, Begampur and Bhangora by the Maharana, and the defeat of the Imperial army under Prince

Akbar at the hands of Maharana's heir apparent Kunwar Jai Singh. The inscription mentions that prince Bhim Singh destroyed one big and thirty small mosques at Ahmedabad. It gives an account of the overtures of peace made by Emperor Aurangzeb, and describes how peace was actually made with an exchange of precious ceremonial gifts.

10. *An inscription in Hinglu Vava*, near Amberi, 7 miles from Udaipur, of the time of Rana Mokal of Mewar. It is engraved on a large slab containing 35 lines. The upper right-hand portion of the inscription is broken off. It is dated the 5th day of the bright half of Jyeshtha, Samvat 1487 (16 May, A.D. 1431) and Shaka 1352. It gives an account of the family of Surpala, a *Gauda* Brahman of Hariyana and his descendants, one of whom, Vidyadhar, built a well in Maharana Mokal's time. The inscription has now been removed to Udaipur.

11. A *Copper Plate Inscription of V.S. 1462* (A.D. 1405) in the possession of Champalal *suthar* (architect) at Udaipur. It states that the architect Mandana had been especially called from Gujarat by Maharana Mokal.

Inscriptions of Maharana Kumbha's Time

(These inscriptions are fully described in Chapter XV of this book, pp. 167–187.)

12. *An inscription*, dated *Kartik Sud* 2, V.S. 1491 (A.D. 1434) with Yati Khemsagar in the village Delwara (Udaipur State). See p. 170.

13. A *copper plate inscription*, dated *Asadh Vad Amavasya*, V.S. 1494 (A.D. 1437) found in the village Nandia, now kept in the Rajputana Museum, Ajmer. See p. 170.

14. *An inscription* dated *Magh Sud* 11, V.S. 1494 (A.D. 1437) on the image of Shantinath in the temple of Adabadanathji in the town of Nagda. See pp. 170–71.

15. *Rānpur Temple Inscription* of A.D. 1439. See p. 171. The complete text of this inscription is published in the Appendix.
16. *An inscription*, dated *Magh Sud 5*, V.S. 1500 (25 January, A.D. 1444) fixed in a wall in a temple near the village of Kadiyān. See p. 173.
17. *Rupaheli Inscription*, dated *Asadh Bad* 1st, V.S. 1505 (A.D. 1448) in a Jain temple. See p. 174.
18-21. *Four Inscriptions*, dated *Magsar Sud* 15th, V.S. 1505 (A.D. 1448) on the images of Shridhara, Krishna Rukmani, Rama, Lakshmana and Madhava Tulsi, in the Chitor Kumbhaswami temple. See p. 174.
22. *Singar Chanvri* Inscription at Chitor, dated A.D. 1448). See p. 175.
23. *Abu Dilwara Temple Inscription*, dated *Asadh Sud* 2, V.S. 1506 (A.D. 1849) See p. 175.
24. An Inscription on a perforated stone window in the second story of the *Kirtisthambha* at Chitor, dated *Phagun Sud* 5, V.S. 1499 (A.D. 1443). See p. 176.
25. *Vasantgarh Jain Temple Inscription*, dated *Magh Sud* II, V.S. 1507 (A.D. 1450). See p. 176.
29-29. Four Inscriptions on images in Kumbhalgarh, dated *Asoj Sud* 3rd, V.S. 1516 (A.D. 1459). See p. 177.
30. The *Kumbhalgarh Inscription*, dated *Magsar Bad* 5, V.S. 1517 (A.D. 1460) found in the Mamadeva Temple, now kept in the Udaipur Museum. See pp. 177-181.
31. The *Chitor Kirtisthambha Inscription*, dated *Magsar Bad* 5th, V.S. 1517 (A.D. 1460). See pp. 181-186.
(The verses of the above two inscriptions—the Kumbhalgarh and the Kirtisthambha inscriptions—to which references have been made in the book are quoted in original in the Appendix, pp. 205-224.)
32. *The Second Kumbhalgarh Inscription* dated *Magsar Bad* 5th, V.S. 1517 (A.D. 1460). See p. 186.
33. *Achalgarh Jain Temple Inscription*, dated *Vaisakh Sud* 4th, S. 1518 (A.D. 1461). See p. 187.